Lecture Notes in Computer Science 13543

More information about this series at https://link.springer.com/bookseries/558

Xinxing Xu · Xiaomeng Li ·
Dwarikanath Mahapatra · Li Cheng ·
Caroline Petitjean · Huazhu Fu (Eds.)

Resource-Efficient Medical Image Analysis

First MICCAI Workshop, REMIA 2022
Singapore, September 22, 2022
Proceedings

Springer

Editors
Xinxing Xu ⓘ
Institute of High Performance Computing
Singapore, Singapore

Dwarikanath Mahapatra ⓘ
Inception Institute of Artificial Intelligence
Abu Dhabi, United Arab Emirates

Caroline Petitjean ⓘ
University of Rouen
Rouen, France

Xiaomeng Li ⓘ
Hong Kong University of Science
and Technology
Hong Kong, China

Li Cheng ⓘ
University of Alberta
Edmonton, AB, Canada

Huazhu Fu ⓘ
Institute of High Performance Computing
Singapore, Singapore

ISSN 0302-9743   ISSN 1611-3349 (electronic)
Lecture Notes in Computer Science
ISBN 978-3-031-16875-8   ISBN 978-3-031-16876-5 (eBook)
https://doi.org/10.1007/978-3-031-16876-5

This Springer imprint is published by the registered company Springer Nature Switzerland AG
The registered company address is: Gewerbestrasse 11, 6330 Cham, Switzerland

Preface

The 1st International Workshop on Resource-Efficient Medical Image Analysis (REMIA 2022) was held on September 22, 2022, in conjunction with the 25th International Conference on Medical Image Computing and Computer-Assisted Intervention (MICCAI 2022). This will be the first MICCAI conference hosted in Southeast Asia. Due to COVID-19, this year it was a hybrid (virtual + in-person) conference.

Deep learning methods have shown remarkable success in many medical imaging tasks over the past few years. However, it remains a challenge that current deep learning models are usually data-hungry, requiring massive amounts of high-quality annotated data for high performance. Firstly, collecting large scale medical imaging datasets is expensive and time-consuming, and the regulatory and governance aspects also raise additional challenges for large scale datasets for healthcare applications. Secondly, the data annotations are even more of a challenge as experienced and knowledgeable clinicians are required to achieve high-quality annotations. The annotation becomes more challenging when it comes to the segmentation tasks. It is infeasible to adapt data-hungry deep learning models to achieve various medical tasks within a low-resource situation. However, the vanilla deep learning models usually have the limited ability of learning from limited training samples. Consequently, to enable efficient and practical deep learning models for medical imaging, there is a need for research methods that can handle limited training data, limited labels, and limited hardware constraints when deploying the model.

The workshop focused on the issues for practical applications of the most common medical imaging systems with data, label and hardware limitations. It brought together AI scientists, clinicians, and students from different disciplines and areas for medical image analysis to discuss the related advancements in the field. A total of 19 full-length papers were submitted to the workshop in response to the call for papers. All submissions were double-blind peer-reviewed by at least three members of the Program Committee. Paper selection was based on methodological innovation, technical merit, results, validation, and application potential. Finally, 13 papers were accepted at the workshop and chosen to be included in this Springer LNCS volume.

We are grateful to the Program Committee for reviewing the submitted papers and giving constructive comments and critiques, to the authors for submitting high-quality papers, to the presenters for excellent presentations, and to all the REMIA 2022 attendees from all around the world.

August 2022

Xinxing Xu
Xiaomeng Li
Dwarikanath Mahapatra
Li Cheng
Caroline Petitjean
Huazhu Fu

Organization

Workshop Chairs

Xinxing Xu	IHPC, A*STAR, Singapore
Xiaomeng Li	Hong Kong University of Science and Technology, Hong Kong, China
Dwarikanath Mahapatra	Inception Institute of Artificial Intelligence, Abu Dhabi, UAE
Li Cheng	ECE, University of Alberta, Canada
Caroline Petitjean	LITIS, University of Rouen, France
Huazhu Fu	Institute of High Performance Computing, A*STAR, Singapore

Local Organizers

Rick Goh Siow Mong	IHPC, A*STAR, Singapore
Yong Liu	IHPC, A*STAR, Singapore

Program Committee

Behzad Bozorgtabar	EPFL, Switzerland
Élodie Puybareau	EPITA, France
Erjian Guo	University of Sydney, Australia
He Zhao	Beijing Institute of Technology, China
Heng Li	Southern University of Science and Technology, China
Jiawei Du	IHPC, A*STAR, Singapore
Jinkui Hao	Ningbo Institute of Industrial Technology, CAS, China
Kang Zhou	ShanghaiTech University, China
Ke Zou	Sichuan University, China
Meng Wang	IHPC, A*STAR, Singapore
Olfa Ben Ahmed	University of Poitiers, France
Pushpak Pati	IBM Research Zurich, Switzerland
Sarah Leclerc	University of Burgundy, France
Shaohua Li	IHPC, A*STAR, Singapore
Shihao Zhang	National University of Singapore, Singapore
Tao Zhou	Nanjing University of Science and Technology, China

Contents

Multi-task Semi-supervised Learning for Vascular Network Segmentation and Renal Cell Carcinoma Classification

Rudan Xiao[1]($\boxtimes$), Damien Ambrosetti[2], and Xavier Descombes[1]

[1] Université Côte d'Azur, Inria, CNRS, I3S, Nice, France
rudan.xiao@inria.fr
[2] Hôpital Pasteur, CHU Nice, Nice, France

Abstract. Vascular network analysis is crucial to define the tumoral architecture and then diagnose the cancer subtype. However, automatic vascular network segmentation from Hematoxylin and Eosin (H&E) staining histopathological images is still a challenge due to the background complexity. Moreover, there is a lack of large manually annotated vascular network databases. In this paper, we propose a method that reduces reliance on labeled data through semi-supervised learning (SSL). Additionally, considering the correlation between tumor classification and vascular segmentation, we propose a multi-task learning (MTL) model that can simultaneously segment the vascular network using SSL and predict the tumor class in a supervised context. This multi-task learning procedure offers an end-to-end machine learning solution to joint vascular network segmentation and tumor classification. Experiments were carried out on a database of histopathological images of renal cell carcinoma (RCC) and then tested on both own RCC and open-source TCGA datasets. The results show that the proposed MTL-SSL model outperforms the conventional supervised-learning segmentation approach.

Keywords: Vascular network segmentation · Semi-supervised learning · Multi-task learning · Renal cell carcinoma

1 Introduction

85% to 90% of kidney cancer are RCC, with the main subtypes being clear cell RCC (ccRCC) with 75%, papillary RCC (pRCC) with 10% and Chromophobe with 5% [11]. Currently, subtyping is essentially based upon pathological analysis, consisting of cell morphology and tumor architecture [8]. [25] proved vascular network analysis is important and relevant in RCC subtyping, however this classification work only used a few manually segmented vascular networks, which limits its application potential. In this paper, we propose to build an automatic vascular network segmentation model paired with a tumor classification scheme.

Data labeling is often the most challenging task. Labeling large-scale images are laborious, time-consuming and exhibit low repeatability. This encouraged to

X. Xu et al. (Eds.): REMIA 2022, LNCS 13543, pp. 1–11, 2022.
https://doi.org/10.1007/978-3-031-16876-5_1

improve the vascular network segmentation performance using unlabeled data. This is indeed the paradigm of SSL models. Compared with the difficulty of obtaining manually a vascular network mask for the segmentation task, the labeling for the classification task is easy to obtain. We conjectured that joint supervised classification and SSL for vascular network segmentation, both embedded in a MTL model, may improve the performance of vascular network segmentation in RCC histopathological images.

We conducted benchmark experiments of supervised learning, SSL, both single and multi-tasks, on RCC histopathological images. Then test on RCC and other types of tumors. The proposed MTL-SSL model performs best, outperforming and more robust than the fully supervised learning model. Moreover, compared with the single-task SSL, our model indeed improves the segmentation efficiency of the vascular network while also performing tumor classification.

Our contributions can be summarized as follows:

- We propose an MTL-SSL model performing joint SSL segmentation and classification tasks to segment the vascular network using both labeled and unlabeled data.
- We apply the first automatic, end-to-end vascular network segmentation method in H&E staining histopathological images, which is robust and outperforms the fully supervised model on both RCC new subtype and other cancer datasets.
- The proposed MTL-SSL model forms a foundation for future developments in multi-task learning dealing with vascular segmentation and classification from H&E staining histopathological images.

2   Related Works

SSL [6] plays a key role in segmentation tasks since it allows to reduce the reliance on large annotated datasets. It can provide an effective way of leveraging unlabeled data to improve model performance. Several approaches have been proposed for SSL, such as Deep Adversarial Networks [27], Cross Pseudo Supervision [7], Cross Consistency Training [15] and Mean Teacher [22]. However, only a few studies have investigated if SSL can be applied to achieve satisfactory results in H&E staining histopathological images, such as NAS-SGAN [9] for atypia scoring of breast cancer, OSE-SSL [19] for content-based image retrieval of prostate cancer, and breast cancer classification with Self-Paced Learning together [2]. In this paper, we apply SSL to RCC histopathological images to provide the benchmarks for vascular network segmentation.

MTL [4] aims at improving the performance of multiple related learning tasks by leveraging comprehensive information among them. MTL achieves better generalization properties than single-task learning. Classification and segmentation are both key tasks in medical image processing. Joint segmentation and classification of tumors in 3D automated breast ultrasound images shows that learning these two tasks simultaneously improves the outcomes of both tasks [28]. Other joint tasks using MTL in algal detection and segmentation [16]. [5] using MTL in cell detection and segmentation on colon rectal cancer images. MitosisNet for mitosis detection from pathological images which consist of segmentation, detection and classification models [1], etc. In this paper, we combine the classification task for which labels are easy to obtain and the vascular network segmentation task for which images have complex backgrounds and manual delineation is cumbersome. Our MTL aims to improve the performance of the segmentation task on RCC histopathological images compared to the fully supervised learning task.

Vasculature from histological images plays a key role in cancer development subtyping and radiotherapy assessment [13]. However, the current automatic vascular segmentation for histopathological images is limited to Immunohistochemistry (IHC) stained histology images. [3] segments and quantify blood vessels from hematoxylin and diaminobenzidine (H&DAB) stained histopathological images of Alzheimer's disease. [12] obtained vascular hotspot probability maps of WSI by scanning whole CD34 immunostained histological images of colon cancer samples. Using H& DAB staining for special coloration of blood vessels, the background is clean and easy to segment, but the background of the H&E image is more complex and has some similar linear structures, such as cell membranes and fibers, etc., which makes the task of vascular segmentation from H&E images more challenging. In this paper, we propose an MTL-SSL model which can segment vascular networks from H&E staining histopathological images automatically while predicting the tumor class.

3   Dataset and Methods

3.1   Dataset Building

We followed the method of [25] to annotate vascular. This weak label is faster and embeds the topological information of the vascular, which has been shown sufficient for the classify subtypes of RCC. Although the width of vascular vessels is lost as we consider to represent the vascular by that way, shown in Fig. 1.

For our own RCC dataset, We collected 167 original H&E staining WSI and labeled the tumor and non-tumor areas using the software ASAP to obtain patches of 2000×2000 Pixels. The pipeline is shown in Fig. 1. We obtain 42130 tumor patches (27287 of ccRCC, 13637 of pRCC, 1206 of Chromophobe), and manually labeled 424 vascular masks (129 of ccRCC, 129 of pRCC, 166 of Chromophobe) for train and test and then labeled 12 masks of Oncocytoma, which is another subtype of RCC, only for test the robustness of the segmentation.

For the TCGA dataset, we downloaded 100 WSIs of RCC (only have ccRCC and pRCC), breast cancer, lung cancer, liver cancer, and esophagus cancer. Then got 1029 tumor patches (433 of RCC, 60 of breast cancer, 246 of liver cancer, 120 of lung cancer, and 170 of esophagus cancer). We manually labeled 90 vascular network masks (20 of RCC, 15 of breast cancer, 20 of liver cancer, 20 of lung cancer, and 15 of esophagus cancer) only for test.

3.2   Multi-task Learning Pipeline

Our proposed MTL-SSL model has a shared backbone encoder with task-specific heads. It consists of a classification task in supervised learning context and a segmentation task using SSL, as shown in Fig. 2. We chose HRNet [20] as the backbone after comparison with other models. HRNet backbone [20] can output high-resolution feature maps. It starts with a high-resolution subnetwork as the first stage, and gradually adds high-to-low resolution subnetworks, forming more stages, and connecting the multi-resolution subnetworks in parallel. HRNet segmentation heads (student and teacher heads) aggregate the output representations at four different resolutions, and then use a 1×1 convolutions to fuse these representations. HRNet classification head fed the four-resolution feature maps into a bottleneck and the number of output channels are increased to 128, 256, 512, and 1024, respectively, and transform 1024 channels to 2048 channels through a 1×1 convolution finally. The codes of Multi-task and HRNet backbone were developed according to the shared repositories [23] and [20]. The main hyperparameters used in our paper are the same as in [23] and [20]. Ensuring fair comparison, all the models were trained using the same hyperparameters.

We chose the Mean Teacher [22] for SSL, which has two neural networks of student and teacher modules sharing the same architecture. Both the student and the teacher module evaluate the input slightly perturbed with Gaussian noise (ξ and ξ') within their computation. The weights of the student module are updated using the Adam optimizer, whereas the weights of the teacher module are the Exponential Moving Average (EMA) of the student weights. We use the cross-entropy (CE) and Dice loss functions between the student's predictions and the ground-truth on the labeled dataset to get *loss2*. The consistency cost, called *loss3* here, is computed from the student's prediction and the teacher's prediction by Mean Square Error (MSE) on the unlabeled dataset. The semi-supervised *loss4* is the sum of the supervised *loss2* and the consistency cost *loss3* by consistency weights, which were taken from [22]. Classification *loss1* is computed by the CE function on the class labeled dataset. Final *loss5* of our MTL-SSL model is the weighted sum of semi-supervised *loss4* and classification *loss1*, we define the weight ratio of SSL and classification as 2:1.

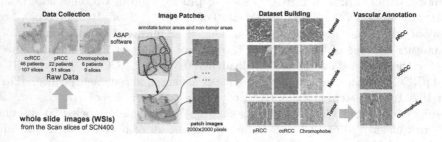

Fig. 1. RCC histopathological images dataset.

3.3   Evaluation

The weakly label of the vascular network has been made with constant width bands [25]. Shown as Fig. 3, the generated vascular segmentation is even closer to the real vascular mask than the weakly labeled ground truth. The classical evaluation indexes such as Dice or Jaccard are not relevant here due to false positive and negative pixels appear at the border of a vessel. To overcome this imprecise ground truth we proposed the following post-processing to evaluate the results in terms of vessel detection, basically to consider length but not the width of vessels. We dilated (with a disk of radius 3, according to Table 1) the segmentation result S to obtain DS and the ground truth GT to obtain DGT. We computed the ratio of miss-detected vessels as:

$$MV = \frac{|\{(i,j) : GT(i,j) = 1, DS(i,j) = 0\}|}{|\{(i,j) : GT(i,j) = 1\}|} \tag{1}$$

and the ratio of falsely detected vessels as:

$$FV = \frac{|\{(i,j) : S(i,j) = 1, DGT(i,j) = 0\}|}{|\{(i,j) : S(i,j) = 1\}|}. \tag{2}$$

Finally, we defined the following global performance index:

$$IV = 1 - (MV + VF)/2 \tag{3}$$

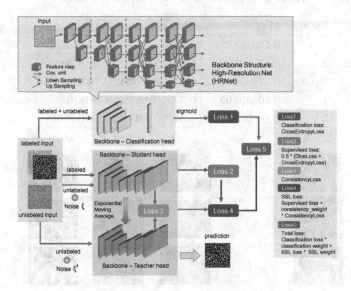

Fig. 2. Proposed MTL-SSL model architecture.

4   Experiments and Results

In this section, we launch the benchmark experiments for vascular network segmentation with different models and also do the statistical analysis of the differences in the results between our proposed model and other models using the student's t-test. The statistical software SPSS, version 20.0, was used for all the statistical analyses. The level for statistical significance was set $\alpha = 0.05$. *: significantly worse than HRNet backbone or our proposed model (P <0.05).

4.1   Backbone and MTL-SSL Method Choice

We conducted experiments on different supervised classification models (GoogLeNet [21], ShuffleNet [26], VggNet [18], ResNet [10] and HRNet [20]) and competitive SSL models (Cross Pseudo Supervision (CPS) [7], Cross Consistency Training (CCT) [15], Entropy Minimization (EM) [24] Deep Co-Training (DCT) [17] and Mean Teacher (MT) [22]) to select the more efficient backbone. For the classification, we split our database into train input with 18624 tumor patch images (8913 of ccRCC, 9079 of pRCC and 632 of Chromophobe), validation with 4843 tumor patch images (2049 of ccRCC, 2523 of pRCC and 271 of Chromophobe), and test with 6973 tumor patch images (4420 of ccRCC, 2250 of pRCC and 303 of Chromophobe). For train input of SSL segmentation, we used both the labeled vascular masks of our dataset with 335 tumor patch images

Table 1. Evaluate with different Strel Radius.

Radius	MV($\downarrow$)	FV($\downarrow$)	IV($\uparrow$)
1	0.1353(0.02)	0.3514(0.06)	0.7566(0.02)*
2	0.1208(0.02)	0.3361(0.06)	0.7716(0.02)*
3 (Our)	0.2798(0.02)	**0.1243(0.03)**	**0.7979(0.01)**
4	0.1040(0.02)	0.3205(0.06)	0.7878(0.02)
5	**0.0835(0.02)**	0.3426(0.04)	0.7870(0.01)

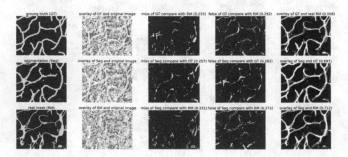

Fig. 3. Calculate the missing part and the false part between the generated segmentations, weakly labels, and real vascular masks by comparing them.

(112 of ccRCC, 111 of pRCC and 112 of Chromophobe) and the 1005 unlabeled data from the RCC dataset randomly, which is 3 times the labeled data. Meanwhile the validation of SSL with 32 tumor patch images (8 of ccRCC, 9 of pRCC and 15 of Chromophobe) and test with 69 tumor patch images (9 of ccRCC, 9 of pRCC, 39 of Chromophobe and 12 of Oncocytoma) selected randomly. All the experiments have been repeated 5 times. The mean and standard deviation of the different model results are shown in Table 2. HRNet backbone performed best in both classification and SSL segmentation tasks. And MTL-SSL based on mean teacher reaches the best performance among all the segmentation methods. All the code and parameters are from the open repository SSL4MIS [14].

Table 2. Performance of different backbones.

Methods		Backbone	Accuracy		
Classification		GoogLeNet	0.9348(0.01)		
		ShuffleNet	0.7753(0.07)*		
		VggNet	0.9114(0.01)		
		ResNet	0.8863(0.03)		
		DenseNet	0.762(0.001)*		
		HRNet	**0.9369(0.03)**		
Method		Backbone	MV(↓)	FV(↓)	IV(↑)
SSL Segmentation	DCT (ECCV 2018)	UNet	0.3770(0.02)	0.7453(0.05)	0.4388(0.02)*
	EM (CVPR 2019)	UNet	0.3340(0.04)	0.7686(0.01)	0.4487(0.02)*
	CCT (CVPR2020) Single	UNet	0.3644(0.03)	0.7474(0.03)	0.4417(0.004)*
	CPS (CVPR 2021) Task	UNet	0.3459(0.01)	0.7467(0.01)	0.4537(0.01)
	MT (NIPS 2017)	UNet	0.3622(0.002)	0.7827(0.002)	0.4275(0.001)*
	DCT (ECCV 2018)	HRNet	0.2926(0.02)	0.7846(0.01)	0.4614(0.004)
	EM (CVPR 2019)	HRNet	0.3049(0.01)	0.7844(0.01)	0.4554(0.01)
	CCT (CVPR2020) Single	HRNet	0.2842(0.02)	0.7951(0.01)	0.4604(0.01)
	CPS (CVPR 2021) Task	HRNet	0.3190(0.02)	0.7733(0.01)	0.4539(0.01)
	MT (NIPS 2017)	HRNet	0.2934(0.02)	0.7932(0.01)	0.4567(0.01)
	DCT (ECCV 2018)	HRNet	0.3032(0.01)	0.1073(0.02)	0.7948(0.01)
	EM (CVPR 2019)	HRNet	0.1307(0.04)	0.2893(0.06)	0.7900(0.01)
	CCT (CVPR2020) Multi	HRNet	0.1562(0.05)	0.4189(0.05)	0.7209(0.05)*
	CPS (CVPR 2021) Task	HRNet	0.2142(0.03)	0.8455(0.01)	0.4702(0.02)*
	MT (NIPS 2017) **Our**	HRNet	0.2798(0.02)	0.1243(0.03)	**0.7979(0.01)**

4.2 Segmentation Benchmarks of Vascular Network

We conducted benchmark experiments on supervised learning, SSL, single segmentation task and MTL. For SSL, the data split ratios were the same as in the backbone choice experiment. For supervised learning, we only used the 335 labeled data for train input, 32 for validation and 69 for test. All the data were selected randomly. For the common parameter setup, the input size was 512×512 pixels, the optimizer was Adam. We used batches of size 8, epoch of 200 and a poly learning rate decay scheme. The initial learning rate was 0.002 and weight decay was 1×10^{-6}. For the parameter setup specific to SSL, the ema decay was

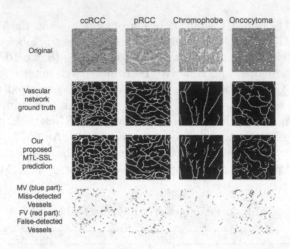

Fig. 4. Segmentation results of the proposed MTL-SSL model.

0.99, the consistency type was "mse", the consistency was 0.1, and the consistency rampup was 50. In addition, we also compare the segmentation results of our MTL-SSL and fully supervised models under different scales of labeled data.

Table 3. Performance of different models.

Supervised	MV(↓)	FV(↓)	IV(↑)
Single-task	**0.2551(0.02)**	0.1600(0.03)	0.7924(0.01)
Multi-task	0.3119(0.05)	**0.1032(0.01)**	0.7925(0.02)
Semi-Supervised	MV(↓)	FV(↓)	IV(↑)
Single-task	0.2934(0.02)	0.7932(0.01)	0.4567(0.01)*
Multi-task (Our)	0.2798(0.02)	0.1243(0.03)	**0.7979(0.01)**

Figure 4 shows the segmentation results of MTL-SSL and Table 3 gives a quantitative evaluation. The proposed MTL-SSL model reaches the best performance among all the experiments. And Table 4 shows the smaller the scale of the labeled data, the more advantages of our MTL-SSL model.

4.3   Test on New Subtype of RCC and Other Cancers Dataset

Figure 5 shows the segmentation results of MTL-SSL on TCGA dataset. And Table 5 shows MTL-SSL model is more robust than fully supervised segmentation when considering new subtype and other cancers test. Our MTL-SSL model appears to be versatile with respect to vascular segmentation tasks, it has the potential to segment vascular from other subtypes of RCC and even other

Table 4. Performance of different labeled data in training.

		Labeled = 200	Labeled = 300	Labeled = all (335)
Supervised	MV($\downarrow$)	**0.091(0.01)**	0.1067(0.02)	**0.2551(0.02)**
Task	FV($\downarrow$)	0.4120(0.02)	0.3670(0.03)	0.1600(0.03)
	IV($\uparrow$)	0.7483(0.01)*	0.7631(0.01)	0.7924(0.01)
Semi-supervised	MV($\downarrow$)	0.1100(0.02)	**0.1046(0.004)**	0.2798(0.02)
Multi-task	FV($\downarrow$)	**0.3580(0.04)**	**0.3302(0.03)**	**0.1243(0.03)**
(Our)	IV($\uparrow$)	**0.7660(0.01)**	**0.7826(0.02)**	**0.7979(0.01)**

Table 5. Performance of new subtype of RCC and other cancers.

Task	Dataset	MV($\downarrow$)	FV($\downarrow$)	IV($\uparrow$)
Supervised task	Our-RCC (new subtype)	**0.1366(0.03)**	0.4501(0.04)	0.7067(0.01)*
	TCGA-RCC (2 subtypes)	0.087(0.01)	0.1746(0.03)	0.8691(0.01)
	TCGA-BRCA (breast)	0.2179(0.05)	0.3892(0.21)	0.6965(0.10)*
	TCGA-LIHC (liver)	0.1720(0.02)	0.3177(0.03)	0.7551(0.02)*
	TCGA-LUSC (lung)	**0.1865(0.02)**	0.2847(0.04)	0.7644(0.02)*
	TCGA-ESCA (esophagus)	0.1734(0.02)	0.2792(0.03)	0.7737(0.01)*
Semi-supervised Multi-task (Our)	Our-RCC (new subtype)	0.1631(0.02)	**0.2635(0.04)**	**0.7867(0.01)**
	TCGA-RCC (2 subtypes)	**0.068(0.01)**	**0.1746(0.02)**	**0.8786(0.01)**
	TCGA-BRCA (breast)	**0.1863(0.03)**	**0.3301(0.1)**	**0.7418(0.03)**
	TCGA-LIHC (liver)	**0.1483(0.03)**	**0.2262(0.08)**	**0.8127(0.03)**
	TCGA-LUSC (lung)	0.1930(0.02)	**0.1910(0.07)**	**0.8080(0.03)**
	TCGA-ESCA (esophagus)	**0.1663(0.02)**	**0.2419(0.08)**	**0.7959(0.03)**

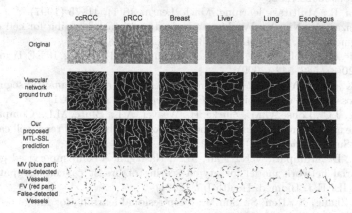

Fig. 5. Segmentation results of the proposed MTL-SSL model on TCGA dataset.

cancers without adding manual vascular masks for training. This provides foundation for the study of the vascular networks in H&E staining histopathological images, which is not limited to immunostaining and manual labeling.

Furthermore, segmentation of vascular networks in H&E histopathology images is very challenging, in this context, our MTL-SSL model has improved state of the art by HRNet backbone, loss strategy, and MTL with classification.

5   Conclusion

The proposed MTL-SSL model, trained with both labeled and unlabeled data, reduces the reliance on manually vascular network masks and achieves automatic segmentation. In our experiments, this model can outperform the fully supervised learning model and is versatile in other types of tumors. That clarified applying the HRNet backbone-based multitask model (jointly with an SSL principle) to vascular segmentation of histopathological images is valuable.

References

1. Alom, M.Z., Aspiras, T., Taha, T.M., Bowen, T., Asari, V.K.: Mitosisnet: end-to-end mitotic cell detection by multi-task learning. IEEE Access **8**, 68695–68710 (2020)
2. Asare, S.K., You, F., Nartey, O.T.: A semisupervised learning scheme with self-paced learning for classifying breast cancer histopathological images. Comput. Intell. Neurosci. **2020** (2020)
3. Bukenya, F., Nerissa, C., Serres, S., Pardon, M.C., Bai, L.: An automated method for segmentation and quantification of blood vessels in histology images. Microvasc. Res. **128**, 103928 (2020)
4. Caruana, R.: Multitask learning. Mach. Learn. **28**(1), 41–75 (1997)
5. Chamanzar, A., Nie, Y.: Weakly supervised multi-task learning for cell detection and segmentation. In: ISBI, pp. 513–516. IEEE (2020)
6. Chapelle, O., Scholkopf, B., Zien, A.: Semi-supervised learning. IEEE Trans. Neural Netw. **20**(3), 542–542 (2009)
7. Chen, X., Yuan, Y., Zeng, G., Wang, J.: Semi-supervised semantic segmentation with cross pseudo supervision. In: CVPR, pp. 2613–2622 (2021)
8. Cheville, J.C., Lohse, C.M., Zincke, H., Weaver, A.L., Blute, M.L.: Comparisons of outcome and prognostic features among histologic subtypes of renal cell carcinoma. Am. J. Surg. Pathol. **27**(5), 612–624 (2003)
9. Das, A., Devarampati, V.K., Nair, M.S.: Nas-sgan: a semi-supervised generative adversarial network model for atypia scoring of breast cancer histopathological images. IEEE J. Biomed. Health Inf. (2021)
10. He, K., Zhang, X., Ren, S., Sun, J.: Deep residual learning for image recognition. In: CVPR, pp. 770–778 (2016)
11. Hsieh, J.J., et al.: Renal cell carcinoma. Nat. Rev. Dis. Primers **3**(1), 1–19 (2017)
12. Kather, J.N., Marx, A., Reyes-Aldasoro, C.C., Schad, L.R., Zöllner, F.G., Weis, C.A.: Continuous representation of tumor microvessel density and detection of angiogenic hotspots in histological whole-slide images. Oncotarget **6**(22), 19163 (2015)
13. Loukas, C.G., Linney, A.: A survey on histological image analysis-based assessment of three major biological factors influencing radiotherapy: proliferation, hypoxia and vasculature. Comput. Methods Program. Biomed. **74**(3), 183–199 (2004)

14. Luo, X.: SSL4MIS. https://github.com/HiLab-git/SSL4MIS (2020)
15. Ouali, Y., Hudelot, C., Tami, M.: Semi-supervised semantic segmentation with cross-consistency training. In: CVPR, pp. 12674–12684 (2020)
16. Qian, P., et al.: Multi-target deep learning for algal detection and classification. In: 2020 42nd Annual International Conference of the IEEE Engineering in Medicine & Biology Society (EMBC), pp. 1954–1957. IEEE (2020)
17. Qiao, S., Shen, W., Zhang, Z., Wang, B., Yuille, A.: Deep co-training for semi-supervised image recognition. In: ECCV, pp. 135–152 (2018)
18. Simonyan, K., Zisserman, Andrew: Very deep convolutional networks for large-scale image recognition. arXiv (2014)
19. Sparks, R., Madabhushi, A.: Out-of-sample extrapolation utilizing semi-supervised manifold learning (OSE-SSL): Content based image retrieval for histopathology images. Sci. Rep. **6**(1), 1–15 (2016)
20. Sun, K., Xiao, B., Liu, D., Wang, J.: Deep high-resolution representation learning for human pose estimation. In: CVPR, pp. 5693–5703 (2019)
21. Szegedy, C., et al.: Going deeper with convolutions. In: CVPR, pp. 1–9 (2015)
22. Tarvainen, A., Valpola, H.: Mean teachers are better role models: weight-averaged consistency targets improve semi-supervised deep learning results. arXiv (2017)
23. Vandenhende, S., Georgoulis, S., Van Gool, L.: MTI-net: multi-scale task interaction networks for multi-task learning. In: Vedaldi, A., Bischof, H., Brox, T., Frahm, J.-M. (eds.) ECCV 2020. LNCS, vol. 12349, pp. 527–543. Springer, Cham (2020). https://doi.org/10.1007/978-3-030-58548-8_31
24. Vu, T.H., Jain, H., Bucher, M., Cord, M., Pérez, P.: Advent: adversarial entropy minimization for domain adaptation in semantic segmentation. In: CVPR, pp. 2517–2526 (2019)
25. Xiao, R., Debreuve, E., Ambrosetti, D., Descombes, X.: Renal cell carcinoma classification from vascular morphology. In: de Bruijne, M., et al. (eds.) MICCAI 2021. LNCS, vol. 12906, pp. 611–621. Springer, Cham (2021). https://doi.org/10.1007/978-3-030-87231-1_59
26. Zhang, X., Zhou, X., Lin, M., Sun, J.: Shufflenet: an extremely efficient convolutional neural network for mobile devices. In: CVPR, pp. 6848–6856 (2018)
27. Zhang, Y., Yang, L., Chen, J., Fredericksen, M., Hughes, D.P., Chen, D.Z.: Deep adversarial networks for biomedical image segmentation utilizing unannotated images. In: Descoteaux, M., Maier-Hein, L., Franz, A., Jannin, P., Collins, D.L., Duchesne, S. (eds.) MICCAI 2017. LNCS, vol. 10435, pp. 408–416. Springer, Cham (2017). https://doi.org/10.1007/978-3-319-66179-7_47
28. Zhou, Y., et al.: Multi-task learning for segmentation and classification of tumors in 3d automated breast ultrasound images. Med. Image Anal. **70**, 101918 (2021)

Self-supervised Antigen Detection Artificial Intelligence (SANDI)

Hanyun Zhang[1,2]([✉]), Khalid AbdulJabbar[1,2], Tami Grunewald[3],
Ayse Akarca[4], Yeman Hagos[1,2], Catherine Lecat[6], Dominic Pate[6], Lydia Lee[6],
Manuel Rodriguez-Justo[6], Kwee Yong[6], Jonathan Ledermann[2,5], John
Le Quesne[7,8,9], Teresa Marafioti[4], and Yinyin Yuan[1,2]

[1] Center for Evolution and Cancer, The Institute of Cancer Research, Sutton, UK
hanyun.zhang@icr.ac.uk
[2] Division of Molecular Pathology, The Institute of Cancer Research, Sutton, UK
[3] University College London Hospital, London, UK
[4] Department of Cellular Pathology, University College London Hospitals,
London, UK
[5] UCL Cancer Institute and UCL Hospitals, Department of Oncology,
University College London, London, UK
[6] Research Department of Hematology, Cancer Institute, University College London,
London, UK
[7] MRC Toxicology Unit, University of Cambridge, Cambridge, UK
[8] Leicester Cancer Research Center, University of Leicester, Leicester, UK
[9] Glenfield Hospital, University Hospitals Leicester NHS Trust, Leicester, UK

Abstract. Multiplexed pathology imaging techniques allow spatially
resolved analysis of cell phenotypes for interrogating disease biology.
Existing methods for cell phenotyping in multiplex images require extensive annotation workload due to the need for fully supervised training.
To overcome this challenge, we develop SANDI, a self-supervised-based
pipeline that learns intrinsic similarities in unlabeled cell images to mitigate the requirement for expert supervision. The capability of SANDI
to efficiently classify cells with minimal manual annotations is demonstrated through the analysis of 3 different multiplexed immunohistochemistry datasets. We show that in coupled with representations learnt
by SANDI from unlabeled cell images, a linear Support Vector Machine
classifier trained on 10 annotations per cell type yields a higher or comparable weighted F1-score to the supervised classifier trained on an average
of about 300–1000 annotations per cell type. By striking a fine balance
between minimal expert guidance and the power of deep learning to learn
similarity within abundant data, SANDI presents new opportunities for
efficient, large-scale learning for multiplexed imaging data.

Keywords: Self-supervised · Multiplexed imaging · Cell classification

---

Supplementary Information The online version contains supplementary material
available at https://doi.org/10.1007/978-3-031-16876-5_2.

1   Introduction

The abundance and spatial location of heterogeneous cell populations in human tissues have been associated with prognosis and response to therapies, highlighting the urgent need to inspect cellular components in the spatial context to better understand their roles during disease progression [3,11,20]. The rapid development of multiplexed imaging techniques such as multiplexed immunohistochemistry (mIHC), multiplexed immunofluorescence and imaging mass cytometry has enabled the spatial distribution of transcripts and proteins to be mapped in situ [12,13,21]. mIHC is more affordable and less restricted by instruments compared to other multiplexed imaging techniques, facilitating its application in large-scale datasets [22]. However, the staining variability, co-expression of antigens, diverse cell morphologies, and cell class imbalance impose unique challenges for cell identification in mIHC images [9].

Existing automated tools for cell identification either use unsupervised algorithms to cluster cells based on color combinations or employ supervised deep learning models using pathologist annotations as training events. Unsupervised methods mainly rely on color decomposition and are often limited to 4–6 color channels [2]. On the other hand, supervised deep learning approaches are less restricted by the color combinations and are capable of identifying cell types meaningful for research and clinical diagnosis, but they require excessive manual labeling to achieve desired performance [1,9].

To leverage the advantages of deep learning and to reduce the annotation burden, we aim to imply intrinsic features from the unlabeled data to facilitate cell classification. In this regard, self-supervised learning serves as an efficient strategy, as the model can learn inherent similarities of unlabeled data free of pre-existing knowledge. For example, a model trained to maximize the agreement between transformations of the same image suffices to distinguish images of different categories [6]. Self-supervised learning has shown great promise in the classification of natural scene images [6,14], hematoxylin and eosin stained slides [7,17], and cell imaging data [16]. However, dedicated approaches for analysing noisy mIHC in patient cohorts are yet to be developed.

Here we propose a pretext task inspired by pathologists' practice of identifying cells in mIHC, which encourages the model to predict the same identity for different views of a cell while dispersing different cells. The model is evaluated across multiple staining combinations and annotation budgets to justify its capability to classify cell types in mIHC slides with minimal human inputs.

2   Method

2.1   Datasets

We collect data from 3 mIHC datasets, including 9 ovarian cancer slides stained with CD8/CD4/FOXP3/PD1, 4 lung squamous cell carcinoma (LUSC) slides with CD8/CD4/FOXP3/haematoxylin, and 6 mycloma slides with

CD8/CD4/FOXP3 (Table 1). Slides are scanned at 40× magnification and down-sampled to 20× before processing. Training and testing datasets are split at the slide level.

Table 1. Composition of the 3 datasets used in the study.

Dataset	Cell classes	No. of cell annotations		Total no. of cell annotations	
		Training	Testing	Training	Testing
Ovarian T cells	CD4+FOXP3+	292	197	1828 (4 slides)	997 (5 slides)
	CD4+FOXP3-	596	168		
	PD1+CD8+	726	347		
	PD1-CD8+	139	203		
	PD1+CD4+	39	60		
	PD1+CD8-CD4-	36	22		
LUSC T cells	CD4+FOXP3+	746	228	2407 (2 slides)	1383 (2 slides)
	CD4+FOXP3-	1225	696		
	CD8+	204	200		
	Haematoxylin-stained	232	259		
Myeloma	CD8+	866	979	3269 (4 slides)	1588 (2 slides)
	CD4+FOXP3-	2244	493		
	CD4+FOXP3+	159	116		

2.2   Single-cell Patches Sampling

All slides are subjected to single-cell detection by a pre-trained deep learning model [19] prior to the proposed pipeline, which predicts cell locations regardless of their classes. To build the dataset for self-learning purposes, the first step is typically to sample single-cell patches from the whole slide image (WSI) [8]. In an ideal scenario where the percentage of cell types present in the dataset is balanced, we can randomly sample from the pool of all detected cells and expect an equal chance of capturing each cell type of interest. However, in pathological data, cell class imbalance is common, which may cause some rare cell types to be missed out by random sampling.

To tackle this problem and to investigate the impact of data imbalance on the model performance, we introduce a data sampling step specifically for multiplex images. Regions on the WSI enriched with diverse cell types are manually selected by a pathologist, to ensure that a considerable number of each cell type are included in the training dataset. Next, a pathologist labels the class of each cell within these regions by dot annotating the cell center using different colors to denote different cell types. We collect manual labels for experimental purpose to reveal the composition of cell types within the regions and provide ground truth for model evaluation (Table 1). A 28 × 28 pixel patch around each dot annotation is retrieved. All patches from slides of the training set are pooled together and randomly allocated for training and validation with a 4:1 ratio.

2.3   Patch Cropping and Pairing

Given a dataset containing n single-cell image patches $D_n = \{x_1, ..., x_n\}$, we first generate all possible combinations $C_2 = \{(x_i, x_j) \in D \mid i \neq j\}$. For each batch, N pairs (x_i, x_j) are randomly sampled from C_2 without replacement. For each pair, the acquired patches x_i, x_j are each randomly cropped into 20×20 pixel sub-patches x_{d_i, s_i} and x_{d_j, s_j}. Sub-patches retrieved from the same patch and the matched patch are labeled as positive P^+ and negative P^- respectively, denoting that they are originated from the same cell or different cells. These are described as follows:

$$P^+ = \{(x_{d_i, s_i}, x_{d_j, s_j}) \in C_2 \mid d_i = d_j, s_i \neq s_j\} \tag{1}$$

$$P^- = \{(x_{d_i, s_i}, x_{d_j, s_j}) \in C_2 \mid d_i \neq d_j, s_i \neq s_j\} \tag{2}$$

The total number of P^+ and P^- in a batch is $2N$ with N set to 256 in the experiment. Image RGB values are normalized to the range (0,1) before feeding to the network (Fig. 1 A). The rationale behind comparing sub-patches randomly cropped from single-cell images is to mimic inspection by pathologists where subtle changes in the field of view should not affect the judgement of cell identities.

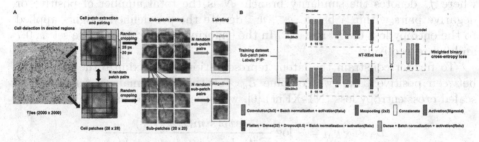

Fig. 1. Schematic to illustrate the SANDI pipeline. A. Data preparation process. Single-cell patches of 28×28 pixel are retrieved from manually picked regions and are randomly paired and cropped into 20×20 pixel sub-patches. Sub-patch pairs originated from the same patch are labeled as positive (P^+), otherwise negative (P^-). B. The Network architecture. Pairs of input sub-patches are processed by two identical encoders to generate a feature vector of 32. The encoded features are concatenated as inputs for the similarity model, which learns to discriminate between similar and dissimilar pairs.

2.4   Network Architecture and Training

A neural network with a double-branch Siamese structure [4] is used to learn representative features of input image pairs that make them similar or disparate (Fig. 1 B). The network consists of two identical encoder branches conjoined at their last layers, followed by a similarity model containing a single branch to compute the similarity metric between the two inputs. Each encoder contained a series of convolution, activation, batch normalization, max-pooling, and dropout layers, which encoded the image into a vector of 32 features. The similarity model concatenates the outputs from two encoders and feeds them through a dense layer, followed by linear activation, batch normalization, Relu activation, and Sigmoid activation to generate a value between 0 and 1, which is interpreted as the predicted similarity score between the image pairs. A higher score indicated more similarity between the two images.

For cell classification purposes, the network is expected to generate a high score for cells from the same class, and a low score for cells from different classes. However, since the network is trained to identify similar or dissimilar pairs randomly sampled from the unlabeled dataset, two images from the same class may have been labeled as negative during data preparation, which biases the network towards features that discriminate against images from the same class. To reduce the impact of this potential bias in negative labels, a weighted binary cross-entropy is used as the loss function:

$$L_{wbce} = -\frac{1}{N} \sum_{i=1}^{N} (w^+ \log(f_s(P_i^+)) + w^- \log(f_s(P_i^-)))$$ (3)

where f_s denotes the similarity branch, N is the total number of positive or negative pairs within a batch. w^+, w^- denote the pre-defined weights applied to the entropy loss of P_i^+ and P_i^-. In the experiment, w^+ and w^- are set as 0.7 and 0.3 respectively.

To further constrain the latent representations to maximize the agreement between positive pairs, we combine L_{wbce} with the normalized temperature-scaled cross entropy loss (NT-XEnt) [6], which is expressed as

$$L_{NT-XEnt} = -\log \frac{exp(sim(z_i, z_j)/\tau)}{\sum_{k=1}^{2N} l_{k \neq i} exp(sim(z_i, z_k)/\tau)}$$ (4)

where z_i and z_j denotes the $l2$ normalized embedding of positive pairs x_{d_i,s_i} and x_{d_i,s_j}, sim denotes cosine similarity, $l_{k \neq i}$ equals to 1 if $k \neq i$, otherwise 0. τ denotes the temperature parameter, which is set as 0.1 in the experiment. For a given sub-patch x_{d_i,s_i}, the NT-XEnt loss treats sub-patches x_{d_i,s_j} as positive samples, and all the other $2N$-2 sub-patches within the batch as negative samples. NT-XEnt is shown to outperform other contrastive loss functions in [6]. The combined loss $L_{combined}$ is the sum of L_{wbce} and $L_{NT-XEnt}$.

All training are performed on an Intel i7-9750H CPU for 100 epochs with a batch size of 256, and optimized using Adam with a learning rate of 10^{-3}. Model with the minimal validation loss is selected for evaluation.

2.5   Reference-based Cell Classification

Identification of cells from multiplex images relies on stain concentrations and cell morphology, which can be affected by experimental artefacts and scanning issues such as out-of-focus. These are known to be major factors influencing model performance in histology image analysis [15,18]. To ensure the quality of cell images while minimizing the need for annotation, we selected a set of reference images $R_n = x_{r_1}, ..., x_{r_n}$ from the training set D as representations of each cell type. Each cell in a hold-out testing set $D_{testing} = x_{q_1}, ..., x_{q_n}$ is treated as a query image x_{q_i}. Both the x_{r_i} and x_{q_i} are cropped into 9 20×20 pixel sub-patches x_{r_i,s_i}, x_{q_i,s_i} and processed by the trained encoder to yield the latent embeddings $f(x_{r_i,s_i})$ and $f(x_{q_i,s_i})$ of size 32×9. Assembling features of sub-patches allow the local regions adjacent to the cell to be incorporated for downstream classification, which has been shown to generate more accurate predictions [19].

To leverage the small reference set, we employ a Support Vector Machine (SVM) classifier with a linear kernel, rather than an additional branch, to categorize cells based on the decision hyperplane optimized for the reference images. To be more precise, the SVM classifier is trained on feature embeddings of references $f(x_{r_i,s_i})$ and predicts cell class for embeddings of unlabeled samples $f(x_{q_i,s_i})$. The SVM classifier is implemented in the libsvm library [5].

2.6   Automatic Expansion of the Reference Set

Although SANDI is able to obtain a considerable accuracy with a limited amount of labels, the classifier trained on a small set of representatives may underestimate the intra-cell-type variations in stain intensities, color combinations and morphologies [9,10,18]. By contrast, a larger training set can expose the model to higher variability in the data, but can also deteriorate model performance if poor-quality data is included [18,23]. An ideal approach to capture a good level of variation while ensuring adequate data quality is to leverage information learnt by self-supervised training to inform the pathologist of cells that are prone to misclassification and thereby, create ground truth feedback to improve model performance. For this purpose, we propose the automatic expansion method for iteratively adding annotations of the least confident instances as training events.

The flowchart illustrating the pipeline is shown in Supplementary Fig. 1. Firstly, we nominate 1 image for each cell class as a representative, forming the initial reference set R_n. Then the minimal Manhattan distance $dist$ between embeddings of unlabeled images xd_i, s_i retrieved from the training set D and that of each reference image x_{r_i,s_i} is used to determine the cell type K. This distance-based classification method is described by:

$$\arg \min_{r_i} P(y \mid dist(f(x_{r_i,s_i}, f(x_{d_i,s_i})))) \tag{5}$$

Second, as an automated reference set expansion, for each group of cells as class K, the cell with the maximum Manhattan distance to any of the reference cells from the same class K is selected and manually labeled. These newly selected cells are then added to the previous reference set, while ignoring repeated instances. The two steps are repeated for 10 rounds, and the weighted F1-score computed on the testing set is examined for each round.

Table 2. Weighted F1-score of SVM classification on testing samples with different percentages of annotation. All results are the average over 5 random trials.

Labeled data	1%	3%	5%	10%	20%	30%	100%
Ovarian T dataset							
Supervised classifier	–	–	–	0.452	0.711	**0.838**	0.856
SimCLR	0.707	0.782	0.789	0.831	0.839	**0.850**	**0.863**
MoCo	0.527	0.671	0.718	0.767	0.776	0.785	0.800
SANDI	**0.820**	**0.817**	**0.829**	**0.845**	**0.853**	0.849	0.846
LUSC T dataset							
Supervised classifier	–	–	–	0.861	0.903	0.890	0.935
SimCLR	0.716	0.757	0.806	0.857	0.880	0.898	0.910
MoCo	0.664	0.725	0.776	0.808	0.827	0.854	0.898
SANDI	**0.883**	**0.886**	**0.887**	**0.898**	**0.916**	**0.922**	**0.934**
Myeloma dataset							
Supervised classifier	–	–	–	0.885	0.930	0.953	0.965
SimCLR	0.879	0.917	0.949	0.953	0.962	0.968	0.982
MoCo	0.844	0.876	0.912	0.928	0.949	0.967	**0.985**
SANDI	**0.912**	**0.942**	**0.952**	**0.965**	**0.975**	**0.977**	0.983

3   Experimental Results

3.1   Classification Performance with Different Size of Randomly Selected Reference Set

To evaluate the performance of SANDI as a function of the size of reference set, we first trained linear SVM classifiers on feature embeddings of randomly sampled training subsets containing 1%, 3%, 5%, 10%, 20%, 30%, and 100% of annotated samples of each cell type. The training of SVM is repeated 5 times on different randomly sampled training sets, and the mean weighted F1-scores are reported on the hold-out testing set containing cells from slides excluded from training. Results are compared against the performance of SVM trained features generated by two state-of-the-art self-supervised methods SimCLR [6] and MoCo [14], and a supervised classifier with the same feature encoder trained on 10%, 20%, 30% and 100% of annotations.

With a budget of 10%, 20% and 30%, SANDI outperforms the supervised classifier, SimCLR and MoCo in all the three datasets. When the budget is reduced to 1%, 3% and 5%, SANDI still achieves a higher or comparable weighted F1-score to the supervised model trained on 10% of annotations. Thus, SANDI can obtain an adequate classification accuracy with 10 times fewer annotations than the conventional supervised training methods.

3.2 Classification Performance with the Automatic Expanding Reference Set

To effectively select reference images to maximize model performance while min-imizing the amount of annotations required, we construct the reference set with iterative model prediction and manual labeling, with the attempt to correct labels for instances with the minimal classification confidence (Sect. 2.6).

The iteration is repeated for 10 rounds. For each iteration, the weighted F1-score of the linear SVM classifier trained on each reference set is evaluated on a constant hold-out testing set (Fig. 2). Example cells classified at the 10th iteration are listed in Supplementary Fig. 2.

We observe an unsteady improvement of the weighted F1-score as the number of references increases, with the highest value occurring before the 10th round. The decrease in accuracy is potentially due to references near the decision bound-ary, which might have mixed-class neighbors and thus cause confusion between adjacent cell classes in the feature space.

Despite the variation in testing accuracy, automatic expanding reference sets at round 10 (with an average of 10 cells per type) yield higher weighted F1-scores than randomly sampled reference sets with about the same number of annotations (3% for Ovarian T and LUSC T, 1% for Myeloma, Table 2). This indicates that selecting the most uncertain cells for annotation effectively boosts the classification accuracy.

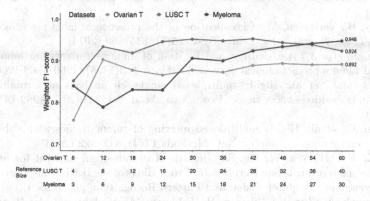

Fig. 2. Weighted F1-score on the testing set for the linear SVM classifier trained on the reference set generated from each round of automatic expansion.

4 Conclusion

We propose a new approach for single cell classification on mIHC images based on self-supervised learning strategy. By employing the prediction of pair-wise similarity as the pretext task, the model leverages intrinsic information from unlabeled data to facilitate the cell classification. The experiment results demonstrate the effectiveness of the proposed pipeline for different combinations of stains, with a minimal number of human annotations required.

References

1. AbdulJabbar, K., et al.: Geospatial immune variability illuminates differential evolution of lung adenocarcinoma. Nat. Med. 1–9 (2020)
2. Bankhead, P., et al.: Qupath: open source software for digital pathology image analysis. Sci. Rep. **7**(1), 1–7 (2017)
3. Bindea, G., et al.: Spatiotemporal dynamics of intratumoral immune cells reveal the immune landscape in human cancer. Immunity **39**(4), 782–795 (2013)
4. Bromley, J., et al.: Signature verification using a "Siamese" time delay neural network. Int. J. Pattern Recognit. Artif. Intell. **07**(04), 669–688 (1993)
5. Chang, C.C., Lin, C.J.: LIBSVM: a library for support vector machines. ACM Trans. Intell. Syst. Technol. **2**(3) (2011). https://doi.org/10.1145/1961189.1961199
6. Chen, T., Kornblith, S., Norouzi, M., Hinton, G.: A simple framework for contrastive learning of visual representations (2020)
7. Ciga, O., Xu, T., Martel, A.L.: Self supervised contrastive learning for digital histopathology. Mach. Learn. Appl. **7**, 100198 (2022)
8. Falk, T.: U-net: deep learning for cell counting, detection, and morphometry. Nat. Methods **16**(1), 67–70 (2019)
9. Fassler, D.J., et al.: Deep learning-based image analysis methods for brightfield-acquired multiplex immunohistochemistry images. Diagn. Pathol. **15**(1), 1–11 (2020)
10. Frénay, B., Verleysen, M.: Classification in the presence of label noise: a survey. IEEE Trans. Neural Netw. Learn. Syst. **25**(5), 845–869 (2014)
11. Galon, J., et al.: Type, density, and location of immune cells within human colorectal tumors predict clinical outcome. Science **313**(5795), 1960–1964 (2006)
12. Gerdes, M.J., et al.: Highly multiplexed single-cell analysis of formalin-fixed, paraffin-embedded cancer tissue. Proc. Natl. Acad. Sci. **110**(29), 11982 LP–11987 (2013)
13. Giesen, C., et al.: Highly multiplexed imaging of tumor tissues with subcellular resolution by mass cytometry. Nat. Methods **11**(4), 417–422 (2014)
14. He, K., Fan, H., Wu, Y., Xie, S., Girshick, R.: Momentum contrast for unsupervised visual representation learning. In: Proceedings of the IEEE Computer Society Conference on Computer Vision and Pattern Recognition, pp. 9726–9735 (2020)
15. Janowczyk, A., Zuo, R., Gilmore, H., Feldman, M., Madabhushi, A.: Histoqc: an open-source quality control tool for digital pathology slides. JCO Clin. Can. Inf. **3**, 1–7 (2019)
16. Kobayashi, H., Cheveralls, K.C., Leonetti, M.D., Royer, L.A.: Self-Supervised Deep Learning Encodes High-Resolution Features of Protein Subcellular Localization. bioRxiv p. 2021.03.29.437595 (2022)
17. Koohbanani, N.A., Unnikrishnan, B., Khurram, S.A., Krishnaswamy, P., Rajpoot, N.: Self-path: self-supervision for classification of pathology images with limited annotations. IEEE Trans. Med. Imaging **40**(10), 2845–2856 (2021)
18. Nalepa, J., Kawulok, M.: Selecting training sets for support vector machines: a review. Artif. Intell. Rev. **52**(2), 857–900 (2019)

19. Sirinukunwattana, K., Raza, S.E., Tsang, Y.W., Snead, D.R., Cree, I.A., Rajpoot, N.M.: Locality sensitive deep learning for detection and classification of nuclei in routine colon cancer histology images. IEEE Trans. Med. Imaging **35**(5), 1196–1206 (2016)

20. Tamborero, D., et al.: A pan-cancer landscape of interactions between solid tumors and infiltrating immune cell populations. Clin. Can. Res. **24**(15), 3717–3728 (2018)

21. Tan, W.C.C., et al.: Overview of multiplex immunohistochem-istry/immunofluorescence techniques in the era of cancer immunotherapy. Cancer Commun. **40**(4), 135–153 (2020)

22. Taube, J.M., et al.: The society for immunotherapy of cancer statement on best practices for multiplex immunohistochemistry (IHC) and immunofluorescence (IF) staining and validation. J. ImmunoTher. Can. **8**(1), e000155 (2020)

23. Tsyurmasto, P., Zabarankin, M., Uryasev, S.: Value-at-risk support vector machine: stability to outliers. J. Comb. Optim. **28**(1), 218–232 (2014)

RadTex: Learning Efficient Radiograph Representations from Text Reports

Keegan Quigley[1(✉)], Miriam Cha[1], Ruizhi Liao[2], Geeticka Chauhan[2], Steven Horng[3], Seth Berkowitz[3], and Polina Golland[2]

[1] MIT Lincoln Laboratory, Lexington, MA, USA
Keegan.Quigley@ll.mit.edu
[2] CSAIL, Massachusetts Institute of Technology, Cambridge, MA, USA
[3] Beth Israel Deaconess Medical Center, Harvard Medical School, Boston, MA, USA

Abstract. Automated analysis of chest radiography using deep learning has tremendous potential to enhance the clinical diagnosis of diseases in patients. However, deep learning models typically require large amounts of annotated data to achieve high performance – often an obstacle to medical domain adaptation. In this paper, we build a data-efficient learning framework that utilizes radiology reports to improve medical image classification performance with limited labeled data (fewer than 1000 examples). Specifically, we examine image-captioning pretraining to learn high-quality medical image representations that train on fewer examples. Following joint pretraining of a convolutional encoder and transformer decoder, we transfer the learned encoder to various classification tasks. Averaged over 9 pathologies, we find that our model achieves higher classification performance than ImageNet-supervised and in-domain supervised pretraining when labeled training data is limited.

Keywords: Multimodal representation learning · Data efficiency

1 Introduction

Automated medical diagnostics from X-ray imagery have the potential to reduce strain on clinicians in hospital settings [6,25], and may even provide rapid insights into patient condition outside of the hospital [2]. Deep learning (DL) and particularly convolutional neural networks (CNNs) have proven to be powerful tools for a wide range of computer vision tasks. Yet despite the advancement of CNNs, automated medical image assessment remains challenged by a lack of the massive expert-labeled datasets needed to successfully train such models. Extracting labels from existing clinical reports provides moderately sized labeled datasets for DL, but the process can be noisy and fails to provide the annotations needed for many high priority clinical tasks. Curating a medical dataset of comparable scale and quality to natural image datasets such as ImageNet (*i.e.*, 1.4 million annotated images) is intractable because manual annotation

X. Xu et al. (Eds.): REMIA 2022, LNCS 13543, pp. 22–31, 2022.
https://doi.org/10.1007/978-3-031-16876-5_3

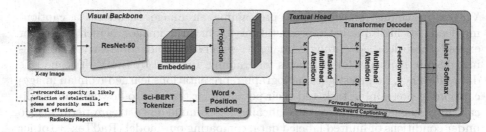

Fig. 1. Overview of our RadTex framework. RadTex consists of a visual backbone based on ResNet-50 and textual head using transformer decoders, jointly trained from scratch on MIMIC-CXR v2.0 X-ray images and radiology reports. Element-wise sum and LayerNorm follow each layer in the transformer decoder, but are omitted from the visualization for simplicity.

of medical images by clinical experts is extremely time-consuming and expensive. In one study, for example, labeling pulmonary edema severity on 141 chest radiographs by 4 radiologists through a consensus process took approximately 25 man-hours [12]. Therefore, efficient learning from limited datasets on the scale of 100 labeled examples will be necessary as research models continue to be developed and implemented in the complex and high-stakes medical domain.

To address this need, there has been increasing interest in adopting pre-training weights, which can be transferred to downstream medical tasks with limited labeled data. A common method transfers model weights from supervised ImageNet-pretraining [30,32], yet there is a considerable gap between the natural image and medical image domains. In response to questions raised about the method's effectiveness in medical contexts [24], some have attempted to bridge the domain gap by pretraining on existing large-scale labeled medical datasets [13]. However, even this type of supervised, in-domain pretraining mostly relies on semantically sparse learning signals; labels are extracted through natural language processing (NLP) on accompanying text reports [14,28], producing large-scale yet noisy annotations [26] not ideal for building efficient representations for transfer learning.

Demonstrating alternatives to supervised pretraining, several recent studies leverage the unlabeled radiology reports for weak supervision. Clinical reports capture physicians' impressions in the form of unstructured text, yet contain rich semantic information. Prior work has capitalized on these natural annotations by using contrastive learning to encourage similar feature representations between image and text [4,21,32]. While these methods attempt to learn representations from images and text jointly, we take a different approach, learning representations by predicting text *from* images. The report generation task is an active area of research [1,9,23], and Wang *et al.* [29] even demonstrated that pretrained LSTM captioning models improve downstream classification of medical images, but efficiency of learned representations for transfer is yet unknown.

In this work, we aim to learn efficient radiograph representations from scratch that train on *fewer* images. Recently, Desai *et al.* [7] introduced the

VirTex framework showing that pretraining an image encoder via captioning leads to high-quality representations of natural images, which match or exceed those learned through ImageNet-supervised and contrastive pretraining, despite requiring fewer images for training. Inspired by the VirTex model's data-efficiency, we investigate radiograph representations learned from an image-captioning pretraining task and their potential for transfer to downstream medical image classification tasks. Specifically, we examine downstream performance under conditions of limited labeled data, comparing our model (RadTex) to other pretrained models. We find that (A) RadTex pretraining outperforms ImageNet and in-domain supervised pretraining methods when fewer than 1000 examples are available for training, (B) decreases in performance of just 0.05 AUC and 0.01 AUCPR are observed for RadTex when training data is reduced from tens of thousands of examples to 100 examples, and (C) pretraining RadTex on in-domain image-text datasets with at least 100K examples is necessary to build transferable and interpretable representations.

2   Method

We aim to use radiology reports to provide weak supervision for learning transferable radiograph representations. Compared to labels or segmentation annotations, radiology reports provide semantically dense information about the contents of a radiograph. Not only do reports note presence or absence of phenomena, but they also describe inter-relatedness between conditions and provide supporting evidence for diagnoses. The recent work of Desai *et al.* [7] exploits the semantic density of text, showing that transferable representations of images can be learned from corresponding textual captions by jointly training an image encoder and text decoder. We adapt the VirTex model to the radiology domain, training an encoder-decoder architecture on MIMIC-CXR v2.0 X-rays and radiology reports [17]. TieNet [29] similarly applied image-captioning to the radiology domain, but in contrast, we train our model from scratch, use transformer decoders for captioning, and explore efficiency of learned representations.

2.1   Network Architecture

Our model, RadTex, closely mirrors the architecture of VirTex with two main components: a visual backbone and textual head (encoder and decoder, respectively). Augmented X-rays are input to a visual backbone, consisting of a ResNet-50 convolutional network and a linear projection layer, which flattens embeddings to allow for decoder attention over visual features. Corresponding radiology reports are normalized, tokenized, and embedded using a learned token and positional embedding. After element-wise sum, layer normalization and dropout, these vector embeddings are passed to the textual head, which uses transformer decoders [27] to predict masked tokens. The decoders use the context of visual features along with prior token predictions to predict the next token in a sequence. Like VirTex, we use bidirectional prediction of tokens during training. An overview of the RadTex model architecture is shown in Fig. 1.

During transfer, the ResNet-50 is extracted from the visual backbone, and a fully connected linear layer is added as a decision head for supervised classification tasks. While we only report downstream classification results here, the linear decision head could be replaced with networks suited to other downstream tasks. We note that non-convolutional encoders, such as Vision Transformers [8,18], could be incorporated into the visual backbone in the place of ResNet.

2.2   Adapting VirTex to the Radiology Domain

Numerous differences exist between the COCO image-text dataset [22] and MIMIC-CXR radiograph-report dataset. X-ray data are grayscale, and distinguishing content is present in small, local regions of the image. In contrast, COCO images are available in RGB, and context is gained by looking at wide regions of the image. We follow Xie *et al.* [31] and alter the first layer of the standard ResNet-50 architecture used in VirTex to accept 1-channel images. We also adjust the size of the input images to 256×256.

Radiology reports use highly technical language specific to the practitioner's domain to convey findings and contain multiple sections, including *Impressions, Findings, Conclusion,* and *Recommendation.* They also often compare findings to a baseline–either a healthy individual or a previous study of the patient–and describe *absence* as well as presence of phenomena (*e.g.*, "No visible pneumothorax"). This is in stark contrast to COCO captions, which use simple language to describe only the important details present in the scene, and avoid speculation or comparison [5]. To address some of these differences, we use a vocab list specific to the scientific domain, *scibert_scivocab_uncased* [3], take text only from the *Findings* section of the report, and lengthen the maximum caption size that the model can accept to 170 tokens (95th percentile of finding section length).

3   Experimental Results

In our experiments, we investigate RadTex's effectiveness in learning visual representations during pretraining and its downstream transfer efficiency compared to other models with the same encoder architecture: randomly initialized ResNet-50, ImageNet-pretrained [11], and ChestX-ray14-pretrained [13,28] (CXR14).

3.1   Datasets

All examples used in RadTex training come from the MIMIC-CXR v2.0 dataset [15], which includes a total of 247,425 pairs of frontal-view chest radiographs and their corresponding radiology reports. Two datasets that label pathologies in subsets of MIMIC-CXR were used for downstream study:
Pathology9 [21]: Binary classification labels for pathology presence from *MIMIC-CXR-JPG* [16], which applied the CheXpert NLP model [14] to label 247,389 images in the MIMIC-CXR v2.0 dataset using their accompanying

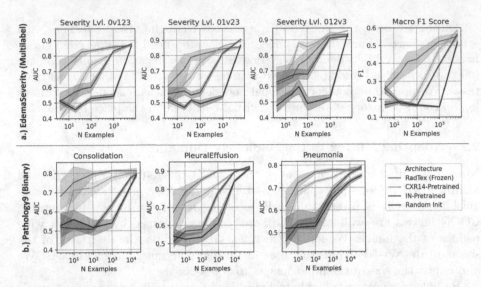

Fig. 2. AUC with a varying amount of labeled training images (N) from a) Edema-Severity and b) Pathology9. We compare frozen RadTex to other initializations, as unfrozen RadTex results were similar. Mean AUC from five trials and 95% confidence interval is shown. Macro F1 score is reported for EdemaSeverity.

reports. We adhere to the official data split as used in Liao *et al.* [21] and train models to classify each pathology individually as positive/negative.

EdemaSeverity [19]: 6,524 examples from MIMIC-CXR with pulmonary edema severity labels (0 to 3, increasing severity) extracted from the radiology reports using a regex model [14,20]. Of these, 141 radiographs were examined by radiologists and consensus was reached on severity level (Fleiss' kappa: 0.42 individually, 0.97 consensus) [12]. We use regex-labeled examples during pretraining and consensus examples during transfer.

3.2 Training Details

To study the efficiency of learned representations, we vary the number of examples in pretraining and downstream datasets and examine the model performance. For each phase of training, we convert images to 1-channel grayscale and perform random affine transformations, keeping the scale of the image constant. For ImageNet- and CXR14-pretrained models, we keep 3-channel inputs to match the pretrained architecture.

Pretraining was done separately for Pathology9 and EdemaSeverity to ensure that the test sets were not seen during pretraining. We pretrain using the same hyperparameters as Desai *et al.* [7], including SGD, LookAhead, and Weight decay. However, we train with a batch size of 128 images across 2 NVIDIA Volta V100 GPUs and do not use an early stopping criterion, but instead pretrain for a full 50 epochs. For pretraining and all downstream training, we use a linear learning rate warmup [10] for 5% of epochs followed by cosine decay for the remaining 95% of training. We pretrain our models and train all downstream models five times to estimate uncertainty in performance.

Table 1. Average AUC/AUCPR for Pathology9 with varying amounts of labeled downstream images. RadTex results use 100% MIMIC pretraining.

Downstream Examples	100%		1000 Ex.		100 Ex.		10 Ex.	
	AUC	AUCPR	AUC	AUCPR	AUC	AUCPR	AUC	AUCPR
Random Init	0.770	0.851	0.628	0.800	0.536	0.751	0.549	0.762
IN-Pretrained	0.763	0.849	0.688	0.820	0.586	0.770	0.555	0.761
CXR14-Pretrained	**0.801**	**0.855**	0.738	0.833	0.688	0.816	0.608	0.797
RadTex Frozen	0.785	0.853	**0.785**	**0.852**	**0.752**	**0.844**	**0.675**	0.817
RadTex Unfrozen	0.762	0.849	0.757	0.843	0.734	0.840	0.670	**0.822**

During downstream training, we use binary cross entropy loss for Pathology9, and cross entropy loss for multi-label EdemaSeverity classification. For all Pathology9 and EdemaSeverity training, we use no weight decay and the same maximum learning rates (LR). In experiments, randomly initialized models ran for 50 epochs, with a max LR of 2×10^{-1}, while all other models were trained for 20 epochs. Through hyperparameter sweeps, the following maximum learning rates were found to be optimal: 2×10^{-3} for IN-Pretrained and RadTex Unfrozen, and 2×10^{-2} for CXR14-pretrained and RadTex Frozen.

3.3 Training with Fewer Labeled Images in Downstream Tasks

Figure 2 compares area under the receiver operating characteristic curve (AUC) values for language-supervised RadTex models, CXR14-pretrained models from [13], ImageNet-pretrained models, and randomly initialized image-only models. We train all models on randomly sampled portions of the downstream training dataset to investigate the relationship between labeled dataset size and performance for each model. Notice that for both EdemaSeverity and Pathology9, RadTex trains representations that transfer to downstream tasks with much more efficiency than other models. When 1000 or fewer examples are available, RadTex matches or outperforms ImageNet- and CXR14-pretrained models.

Table 1 presents averaged AUC and area under the precision-recall curve (AUCPR) results across Pathology9. These findings suggest that RadTex is a promising approach to overcoming the challenge of limited labeled data, commonly found in the medical domain. Crucially, we found that RadTex Frozen performance on 100 labeled examples (AUC/AUCPR: 0.752/0.844) was nearly as good as the top performing model with 100% labeled data (0.801/0.855), where ~100 is a reasonably sized dataset to ask physicians to annotate.

As shown in both Fig. 2 and Table 1, all models perform similarly when all downstream data is used (100% downstream). This is not unexpected–all classification models use the exact same architecture (ResNet-50 with decision head), and thus have the same predictive capacity. Given enough training data and epochs, we would expect performance to converge. However, when training data is limited, the RadTex initialization of models becomes advantageous.

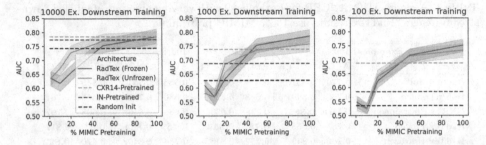

Fig. 3. Averaged Pathology9 AUCs after training on 10K, 1K and 100 downstream examples vs. pretraining dataset (MIMIC-CXR) size.

3.4   Pretrained Representation Quality

While it is intuitive that pretraining with more examples would produce better visual embeddings and representations, we wanted to understand whether the size of the MIMIC-CXR corpus (~250K frontal X-ray/report pairs) was sufficient for the captioning pretraining task. In Fig. 3, we capture the effect of reducing the size of the pretraining set by transferring models to 10K, 1K, and 100 example downstream training on Pathology9. We observe that pretraining with a dataset size 50% of the MIMIC corpus degrades downstream AUCs only slightly compared to the full pretraining set (100 example Pathology-9 drops by 0.03 AUC), yet pretraining with smaller datasets yields significantly worse performance, as the model seems unable to "recover" from a poor initialization. Noting that 50% MIMIC pretraining (~125K examples) represents an inflection point in RadTex downstream performance in Fig. 3, and that VirTex similarly used a pretraining dataset with 118K examples, we recommend that a pretraining dataset of at least 100K examples be available for those looking to apply RadTex to additional radiographic modalities or imaged regions.

3.5   Proxy Task: Generating Radiology Reports

Generating high-quality captions is not the goal of the VirTex or RadTex models, but the task provides interpretability and insight into the representations learned during pretraining. We experimented with radiology report generation in RadTex on the Pathology9 test set after pretraining on MIMIC-CXR. Following 200 epochs pretraining, we apply a beam search algorithm (2 beams) to predict tokens sequentially. As shown in Fig. 4, RadTex-generated reports for three random radiographs from the test set show some agreement with the *Findings* section of the corresponding report. However, while radiology reports build up evidence for diagnoses, these generated reports offer little supporting evidence, and occasionally even refer to information beyond what could be obtained from the image (*e.g.*, "PA lateral views of the chest provided"). Nonetheless, similarities in pathology mentions between generated and written reports suggest that the model is doing more than mimicking the language of radiologists.

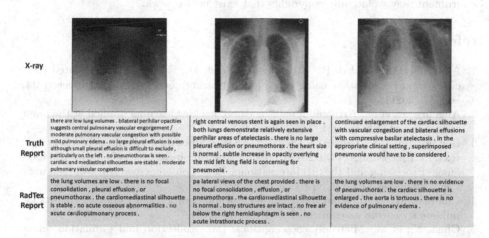

Fig. 4. RadTex-generated reports (*Findings*) compared to the originals.

4   Conclusions

We present a model, RadTex, which leverages the semantic density of radiology reports to build efficiently transferable radiograph representations. We focus our analysis of the model on the effects of data availability, yielding insights into performance on expert-annotated datasets of reasonable curation size according to our clinical collaborators. By adopting radiology report generation as language-supervised pretraining, we observe that the learned image encoder can produce high-quality chest X-ray representations with as few as 100 labeled images, potentially reducing the labeling burden on radiologists for developing deep learning models. Results on various classification tasks suggest that RadTex is a superior approach to supervised pretraining for data-efficient transfer and interpretability. Additionally, our results suggest that pretraining on a large image-text corpus is important to achieving RadTex's competitive advantage.

Acknowledgements. This work was supported in part by MIT Lincoln Laboratory, US Air Force, NIH NIBIB NAC P41EB015902, Wistron, IBM Watson, MIT Deshpande Center, and MIT J-Clinic.

DISTRIBUTION STATEMENT A. Approved for public release. Distribution is unlimited. This material is based upon work supported by the Old Program 1 under

Air Force Contract No. FA8702-15-D-0001. Any opinions, findings, conclusions or recommendations expressed in this material are those of the author(s) and do not necessarily reflect the views of the Old Program 1. ©Massachusetts Institute of Technology. Delivered to the U.S. Government with Unlimited Rights, as defined in DFARS Part 252.227-7013 or 7014 (Feb 2014). Notwithstanding any copyright notice, U.S. Government rights in this work are defined by DFARS 252.227-7013 or DFARS 252.227-7014 as detailed above. Use of this work other than as specifically authorized by the U.S. Government may violate any copyrights that exist in this work.

References

1. Alfarghaly, O., Khaled, R., Elkorany, A., Helal, M., Fahmy, A.: Automated radiology report generation using conditioned transformers. Inf. Med. Unlocked **24**, 100557 (2021)
2. Angehrn, Z., et al.: Artificial intelligence and machine learning applied at the point of care. Front. Pharmacol. **11**, 759 (2020)
3. Beltagy, I., Lo, K., Cohan, A.: SciBERT: a pretrained language model for scientific text. In: Proceedings of the 2019 Conference on Empirical Methods in Natural Language Processing and the 9th International Joint Conference on Natural Language Processing (EMNLP-IJCNLP) (2019)
4. Chauhan, G., et al.: Joint modeling of chest radiographs and radiology reports for pulmonary edema assessment. In: MICCAI (2020)
5. Chen, X., et al.: Microsoft coco captions: Data collection and evaluation server (2015). arXiv:1048550/ARXIV.1504.00325
6. Davenport, T., Kalakota, R.: The potential for artificial intelligence in healthcare. Future Healthcare J. **6**(2), 94 (2019)
7. Desai, K., Johnson, J.: VirTex: learning visual representations from textual annotations. In: CVPR (2021)
8. Dosovitskiy, A., et al.: An image is worth 16x16 words: transformers for image recognition at scale. arXiv (2020)
9. Gasimova, A., Montana, G., Rueckert, D.: Automated knee x-ray report generation. arXiv (2021)
10. Goyal, P., Mahajan, D., Gupta, A., Misra, I.: Scaling and benchmarking self-supervised visual representation learning. CoRR (2019)
11. He, K., Zhang, X., Ren, S., Sun, J.: Deep residual learning for image recognition. CoRR arXiv:abs/1512.03385 (2015)
12. Horng, S., Liao, R., Wang, X., Dalal, S., Golland, P., Berkowitz, S.J.: Deep learning to quantify pulmonary edema in chest radiographs. Radiol. Artif. Intell. **3**(2), e190228 (2021)
13. Hosseinzadeh Taher, M.R., Haghighi, F., Feng, R., Gotway, M.B., Liang, J.: A systematic benchmarking analysis of transfer learning for medical image analysis. In: Albarqouni, S., et al. (eds.) DART/FAIR -2021. LNCS, vol. 12968, pp. 3–13. Springer, Cham (2021). https://doi.org/10.1007/978-3-030-87722-4_1
14. Irvin, J., et al.: Chexpert: a large chest radiograph dataset with uncertainty labels and expert comparison. In: Thirty-Third AAAI Conference on Artificial Intelligence (2019)
15. Johnson, A., et al.: Mimic-cxr, a de-identified publicly available database of chest radiographs with free-text reports. In: Scientific data (2019)
16. Johnson, A., et al.: MIMIC-CXR-JPG - chest radiographs with structured labels (2019)

17. Johnson, A., Pollard, T., Mark, R., Berkowitz, S., Horng, S.: MIMIC-CXR database. PhysioNet (2019)
18. Krishnan, K.S., Krishnan, K.S.: Vision transformer based COVID-19 detection using chest x-rays. In: 2021 6th International Conference on Signal Processing, Computing and Control (ISPCC), IEEE (2021)
19. Liao, R., Chauhan, G., Golland, P., Berkowitz, S., Horng, S.: Pulmonary edema severity grades based on MIMIC-CXR (version 1.0.1). In: PhysioNet (2021). https://doi.org/10.13026/rz5p-rc64
20. Liao, R., Chauhan, G., Golland, P., Berkowitz, S., Horng, S.: Pulmonary edema severity grades based on mimic-cxr (version 1.0.1). PhysioNet (2021)
21. Liao, R., et al.: Multimodal representation learning via maximization of local mutual information. In: MICCAI (2021)
22. Lin, T.Y., et al.: Microsoft coco: Common objects in context (2014). arxiv:1048550/ARXIV.1405.0312
23. Miura, Y., Zhang, Y., Tsai, E.B., Langlotz, C.P., Jurafsky, D.: Improving factual completeness and consistency of image-to-text radiology report generation. arXiv (2020)
24. Raghu, M., Zhang, C., Kleinberg, J., Bengio, S.: Transfusion: Understanding transfer learning for medical imaging. arXiv (2019)
25. Sutton, R., Pincock, D., Baumgart, D., Sadowski, D., Fedorak, R., Kroeker, K.: An overview of clinical decision support systems: benefits, risks, and strategies for success. NPJ Digital Med. 3(1), 1–10 (2020)
26. Thian, Y.L., et al.: Deep learning systems for pneumothorax detection on chest radiographs: a multicenter external validation study. Radiol. Artif. Intell. 3(4), e200190 (2021)
27. Vaswani, A., et al.: Attention is all you need. arXiv (2017)
28. Wang, X., Peng, Y., Lu, L., Lu, Z., Bagheri, M., Summers, R.M.: Chestx-ray8: Hospital-scale chest x-ray database and benchmarks on weakly-supervised classification and localization of common thorax diseases. CoRR arXiv:abs/1705.02315 (2017)
29. Wang, X., Peng, Y., Lu, L., Lu, Z., Summers, R.M.: Tienet: text-image embedding network for common thorax disease classification and reporting in chest x-rays. CoRR arXiv:abs/1801.04334 (2018)
30. Wen, Y., Chen, L., Deng, Y., Zhou, C.: Rethinking pre-training on medical imaging. J. Vis. Commun. Image Representation 78, 103145 (2021)
31. Xie, Y., Richmond, D.: Pre-training on grayscale imagenet improves medical image classification. In: Leal-Taixé, L., Roth, S. (eds.) Computer Vision - ECCV 2018 Workshops (2019)
32. Zhang, Y., Jiang, H., Miura, Y., Manning, C.D., Langlotz, C.P.: Contrastive learning of medical visual representations from paired images and text. arXiv (2020)

Single Domain Generalization via Spontaneous Amplitude Spectrum Diversification

Yuexiang Li[✉], Nanjun He, and Yawen Huang

Tencent Jarvis Lab, Shenzhen, China
vicyxli@tencent.com

Abstract. Due to the domain shift problem, the deep learning models trained on one domain often fail to generalize well on others. Researchers formulated such a realistic-yet-challenging scenario as a new research line, termed single domain generalization (single-DG), which aims to generalize a model trained on single source domain to multiple target domains. The existing single-DG approaches tried to address the problem by generating diverse samples using extra trainable network modules. However, due to the limited amount of medical data, the extra network parameters are difficult to train. The generated samples are often failed to achieve satisfactory effect for improving model generalization. In this paper, we propose a simple-yet-effective Fourier-based approach, which augments data via spontaneous Amplitude SPECTrum diverSification (ASPECTS), for single domain generalization. Concretely, the proposed approach first converts the image into frequency domain using the Fourier transform, and then spontaneously generates diverse samples by editing the amplitude spectrum using a pool of randomization operations. The proposed approach is established upon the assumption that the high-level semantic information (domain-invariant) is embedded in the phase spectrum of images after Fourier transform, while the amplitude spectrum mainly contains the domain-variant information. We evaluate the proposed ASPECTS approach on both publicly available and private multi-domain datasets. Compared to the existing single-DG approaches, our method is much easier to implement (*i.e.,* without training of extra network modules) and yields the superior improvement.

Keywords: Single domain generalization · Data augmentation · Frequency domain

1 Introduction

The effectiveness of deep learning models has been validated for the scenario that the source and target samples are captured from the similar distribution. However, this scenario is difficult to maintain in practice. Medical images from multicentres are usually captured under different imaging conditions, which leads to a gap between source and target domains (known as the *domain shift* problem). Thus, a significant performance degradation is often observed while testing deep learning models trained on the source domains on the discrepant target ones.

Domain adaptation (DA) and domain generalization (DG) are two potential solutions for the domain shift problem. Concretely, DA approaches [2,15,18,21] alleviate the problem by transferring the knowledge extracted from annotated source samples to the unlabeled target ones, which require the availability of both source and target data for network training. For example, Xie *et al.* [15] proposed a DA framework, which achieved knowledge transfer by maximizing the mutual information between source and target domains. Although existing DA approaches provide impressive performance on alleviating domain shift problem, such a setting limits the practical application of DA methods, since the target domains may be inaccessible due to privacy concerns of medical data. In this regard, various DG approaches, which exclude the target samples in the training phase, have been proposed in recent studies [3,6,23]. For example, Zhou *et al.* [23] augmented the source domains by generating synthesized pseudo-novel domain data to boost the model generalization on unseen target domain. The common domain generalization [16] aims to generalize deep learning models to one unseen target domain via jointly learning from multiple source domains. However, considering the privacy of medical data, the requirement of multiple source domains is difficult to fulfill in practice.

To address the previously mentioned privacy problems, researchers formulated a realistic-yet-challenging scenario as a new research line, termed single domain generalization (single-DG), which aims to generalize a model trained on single source domain to multiple target domains. The setting of single accessible source domain makes the prior multi-source DG approaches fail to deal with the single-DG scenario [14]. Therefore, single-DG is still an under-explored area with very limited explorations [11,14,22]. Specifically, Qiao *et al.* [11] constructed a Wasserstein auto-encoder to create adversarial samples for source domain augmentation. Following this direction, Zhao *et al.* [22] proposed a regularization term for the more effective adversarial data augmentation based on information bottleneck principle. In a more recent study, Wang *et al.* [14] proposed an approach, namely learning-to-diversify (L2D), to improving the diversity of adversarial samples. The proposed approach involved a multi-branch style-complement module, which ensures the diversity by gradually enlarging the shift between the distributions of synthesized and source samples. All the existing single-DG approaches share a common drawback—an extra network/module needs to be trained for adversarial sample generation. This drawback limits the application of the existing single-DG approaches to multicentre medical images, since the amount of labeled source medical data may be insufficient for well training of an extra network.

Inspired by the recent multi-source DG method [16], which improves the diversity of training set by mixing the frequency components of samples from different source domains, we propose an intuitive Fourier-based approach, which generates adversarial data via spontaneous Amplitude SPECTrum diverSifica-

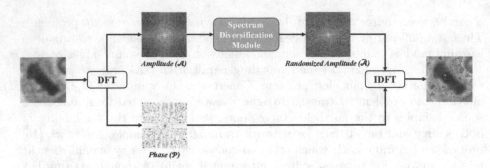

Fig. 1. The pipeline of our ASPECTS. Since the domain-variant information is mainly contained in the amplitude spectrum, we propose a specturm diversification module to edit the amplitude spectrum for adversarial sample generation.

tion (ASPECTS), for single domain generalization. In particular, the proposed approach first converts the image into the frequency domain using the Fourier transform, and then spontaneously generates diverse samples by editing the amplitude spectrum using a pool of randomization operations. The proposed approach is established upon the assumption that the high-level semantic information (domain-invariant) is involved in the phase spectrum of images after Fourier transform, while the amplitude spectrum mainly contains the domain-variant information. We evaluate the proposed ASPECTS approach on both publicly available and private multi-domain datasets. Compared to the existing single-DG approaches, our method is much easier to implement (*i.e.,* without training of extra network modules) and yields the superior improvement. To our best knowledge, this is the first work adapting the single-DG setting for multicentre medical images, which can be seen as a benchmark for the future research.

2   Method

Currently, the assumption that the high-level semantic information (domain-invariant) is involved in the phase spectrum of images after Fourier transform, while the amplitude spectrum mainly contains the domain-variant information has been verified by existing studies [4,9,10,16]. In this regard, we propose an intuitive Fourier-based data augmentation approach, which generates adversarial data via spontaneous Amplitude SPECTrum diverSification (ASPECTS), to improve the model generalization using single source domain. The pipeline is presented in Fig. 1. We first transform the image to frequency space using discrete Fourier transform (DFT) and then randomize the amplitude spectrum using a spectrum diversification module. After that, the phase spectrum is combined with the randomized amplitude for the generation of adversarial samples.

Data Augmentation *vs.* Single-DG. We notice that both data augmentation and single-DG aim to augment the training set to obtain a robust deep learning network; hence it is worthwhile to emphasize the difference between these

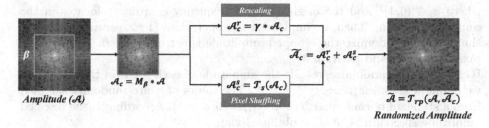

Fig. 2. The proposed *spectrum diversification module* consists of two operations (*i.e.*, rescaling and pixel shuffling) to randomize the amplitude and position of points in amplitude spectrum, respectively.

two areas. Concretely, the goal of data augmentation is to prevent overfitting on the training set and improve the generalization of the trained model on the test set from the same domain. The synthesized images (*e.g.*, by cropping and rotation) are visually similar to the source domain. Single-DG generates samples to improve the generalization of the model on unseen target domains. The synthesized images may be visually different to those in the source domain (refer to Fig. 3).

Discrete Fourier Transformation. Since the proposed ASPECTS is mainly built upon the discrete Fourier transform, we first briefly introduce the DFT. Given an image $x \in \mathbb{R}^{H \times W}$, where H and W are image height and width, respectively, the discrete Fourier transform $\mathcal{F}(\cdot)$ can be formulated as:

$$\mathcal{F}(x) = \sum_{h=0}^{H-1} \sum_{w=0}^{W-1} x(h, w) e^{-j2\pi\left(\frac{h}{H}u + \frac{w}{W}v\right)}, \tag{1}$$

where (u, v) is the coordinate in frequency space. Accordingly, the amplitude and phase spectrums can be expressed as:

$$\mathcal{A}(u, v) = \left[R^2(u, v) + I^2(u, v) \right]^{1/2}, \quad \mathcal{P}(u, v) = \arctan\left[\frac{I(u, v)}{R(u, v)} \right], \tag{2}$$

where $R(\cdot)$ and $I(\cdot)$ are the real and imaginary parts of $\mathcal{F}(\cdot)$. The inverse discrete Fourier transform (IDFT), which transforms amplitude and phase spectres back to the image space, is denoted as $\mathcal{F}^{-1}(\cdot)$.

2.1 Spectrum Diversification Module

The pipeline of our spectrum diversification module is shown in Fig. 2. Concretely, after we obtain the amplitude spectrum $\mathcal{A}$, the low-frequency component is cropped using a mask M_β, which is consistent to [19]:

$$M_\beta(u, v) = \mathbb{1}_{(u,v) \in [-\beta\frac{H}{2} : \beta\frac{H}{2}, -\beta\frac{W}{2} : \beta\frac{W}{2}]}, \tag{3}$$

where $\beta \in (0,1)^1$ and the origin $(0,0)$ of frequency coordinate locates in the centre of spectrum. Then, we implement two operations (*i.e.*, rescaling and pixel shuffling) to randomize the cropped amplitude spectrum ($\mathcal{A}_c$) in terms of the pixel amplitude and position.

Rescaling. To randomize/rescale the amplitude of each point in the spectrum, we define a mask matrix $\gamma \in \mathbb{R}^{\beta H \times \beta W}$. The values of γ are randomly sampled from a standard normal distribution $\mathcal{N}(\mu = 0, \sigma = 1)$. Accordingly, the rescaled amplitude spectrum $\mathcal{A}_c^r$ can be obtained via:

$$\mathcal{A}_c^r(u,v) = \mathcal{A}_c(u,v) * \gamma(u,v). \tag{4}$$

Pixel Shuffling. Since the rescaling operation maintains the primary distribution of $\mathcal{A}_c$, to further randomize the spectrum and accordingly generate the more diverse samples, we perform the pixel shuffling operation (denoted as $\mathcal{T}_s(\cdot)$), which varies the positions of points in the spectrum, to the cropped amplitude spectrum. The shuffled spectrum $\mathcal{A}_c^s$ can be written as: $\mathcal{A}_c^s = \mathcal{T}_s(\mathcal{A}_c)$.

Randomized Spectrum Fusion. With the rescaled spectrum $\mathcal{A}_c^r$ and shuffled spectrum $\mathcal{A}_c^s$, we can obtain the randomized cropped amplitude spectrum $\tilde{\mathcal{A}}_c$ via pixel-wise summation:[2]

$$\tilde{\mathcal{A}}_c = \mathcal{A}_c^r + \mathcal{A}_c^s. \tag{5}$$

To produce the final randomized amplitude spectrum $\tilde{\mathcal{A}}$ for adversarial sample generation, we use $\tilde{\mathcal{A}}_c$ to replace the original $\mathcal{A}_c$ in $\mathcal{A}$. Denoting the spectrum replacing operation as $\mathcal{T}_{rp}(\cdot)$, the generation process can be formulated as $\tilde{\mathcal{A}} = \mathcal{T}_{rp}(\mathcal{A}, \tilde{\mathcal{A}}_c)$.

2.2   Adversarial Sample Generation

A new Fourier representation can be formed by combining the original phase spectrum $\mathcal{P}(x)(u,v)$ and the randomized amplitude spectrum $\tilde{\mathcal{A}}(u,v)$:

$$\mathcal{F}(\tilde{x}) = \tilde{\mathcal{A}}(u,v) * e^{-j*\mathcal{P}(u,v)}, \tag{6}$$

which is then transformed back to the image space using inverse discrete Fourier transform to generate the adversarial sample $\tilde{x} = \mathcal{F}^{-1}(\mathcal{F}(\tilde{x}))$.

3   Experiments

In this section, we validate the effectiveness of our ASPECTS on three datasets, including public (corrupted CIFAR-10 [7] and MIDOG [1]) datasets and private multicentre colposcopic image dataset, and present the experimental results.

---

[1] Note that the hyperparameter β varies in the interval $(0,1)$ during the network training to increase the diversity of adversarial samples.

[2] We notice that there are other ways to fuse the two spectra, *e.g.*, pixel-wise multiplication ($\mathcal{A}_c^r \times \mathcal{A}_c^s$) or series concatenation ($\mathcal{T}_s(\mathcal{A}_c^r)$). However, these fusion approaches are observed to under-randomize the amplitude spectrum and degrade the diversity of adversarial samples. Hence, we adopt pixel-wise summation in this study.

Corrupted CIFAR-10. The publicly available CIFAR-10 [7] and corrupted CIFAR-10 (CIFAR-10-C) [5] are adopted as source and target domains, respectively. Similar to [14], deep learning models are trained on the CIFAR-10 training set, and validated on the CIFAR-10 test set. The generalization performance of well-trained models are then evaluated on CIFAR-10-C, which is a benchmark dataset for the evaluation of model robustness, consisting of 19 corruption types from four categories (*i.e.,* weather, blur, noise and digits). In our experiment, each corruption type is seen as a target domain.

MIDOG. The mitosis domain generalization (MIDOG) dataset [1] consists of human breast cancer tissue samples acquired using four different whole slide image scanners: Hamamatsu XR nanozoomer 2.0 (S1), Hamamatsu S360 (S2), Aperio ScanScope CS2 (S3) and Leica GT450 (S4). Each scanner captured around $1,500$ samples, which can be classified to two categories, *i.e.,* mitotic and negative. Different scanners are seen as different domains in the experiments. Since the annotations are only provided for S1 to S3, S4 is excluded in experiments.

Multicentre Colposcopic Images. We form a multicentre dataset by collecting colposcopic images from six centres. Specifically, we collect $10,000$ samples from centre #1 and $1,000$ samples from each of rest centres (#2 to #6). Hence, the data from centre #1 (source domain) is separated to training and validation sets according to the ratio of 80:20, and the well-trained models are evaluated on the centres #2 to #6 (target domains), respectively. The dataset has the image-level labels (*i.e.,* clinical diagnosis for cervical cancer—abnormal/normal).

Baseline & Evaluation Criterion. We train a model with a pool of data augmentation operations (*e.g.,* rotation and flipping) on the source domain, which serves as the baseline.[3] The average classification accuracy (ACC) is adopted as metric for the performance evaluation.

3.1 Performance Evaluation

In this section, we first compare our ASPECTS with state-of-the-art single-DG [11,13,14] and DG [8,17] approaches on single-DG benchmark CIFAR-10-C dataset.[4] Then, the proposed ASPECTS is further compared with the most competitive single-DG approach (*i.e.,* L2D [14]) on the two medical image datasets for performance evaluation. Adversarial samples yielded by our ASPECTS are shown in Fig. 3. It can be observed that the proposed ASPECTS effectively expands the appearance distribution of source data.

Comparison on CIFAR-10-C. For a fair comparison, the same backbone to [14] (*i.e.,* WideResNet(16-4) [20]) is adopted in our study for the experiments on CIFAR-10-C, and all models are trained under the same protocol [14]. The single domain generalization accuracies yielded by different approaches on

---

[3] Note that the same data augmentation operations are adopted to train benchmarking algorithms and our ASPECTS.

[4] Consistent to [14], DG approaches can access multiple source domains for training.

38   Y. Li et al.

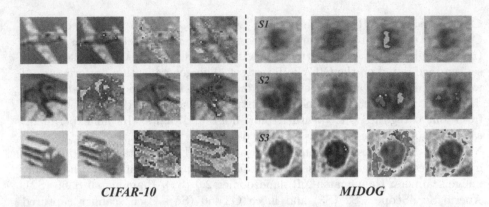

CIFAR-10   MIDOG

Fig. 3. Visualization of adversarial samples generated by our ASPECTS. The first column of each dataset shows the original samples, and the corresponding adversarial samples are presented in the second to fourth columns. Due to the data privacy, we do not visualize the diversified samples for colposcopic images.

Table 1. Single domain generalization accuracy (%) on CIFAR10-C [5]. The model is trained on clean CIFAR10 data [7] and tested on CIFAR10-C. The ACC (%) of 19 types of corruption at the severest level is evaluated (only eight corruptions are listed in the table). The column 'Mean' shows the mean accuracy on all 19 corruptions.

	Weather		Blur		Noise		Digits		Mean
	Fog	Frost	Zoom	Defocus	Speckle	Impulse	Pixelate	Spatter	
Baseline	65.92	61.57	59.97	53.71	41.31	25.65	41.07	75.36	56.15
CCSA [8]	66.94	61.49	61.96	56.11	40.12	24.56	40.94	77.91	56.31
d-SNE [17]	65.99	75.46	58.47	53.71	45.30	27.95	38.46	73.40	56.96
GUD [13]	68.29	69.94	62.95	56.41	38.45	22.26	53.34	80.27	58.26
M-ADA [11]	69.36	**76.66**	68.04	61.18	60.88	45.18	52.25	80.62	65.59
L2D [14]	73.37	71.56	75.53	79.03	**63.05**	64.75	72.33	79.33	72.77
ASPECTS	**75.46**	73.34	**80.01**	**80.39**	61.54	**74.10**	**73.90**	**82.31**	**74.28**

CIFAR-10-C are presented in Table 1. Single-DG approaches (*i.e.*, GUD, M-ADA, L2D and our ASPECTS) are observed to achieve promising ACCs, which are even better than the DG methods (*i.e.*, CCSA and d-SNE) with the access of multiple source domains. Specifically, our ASPECTS achieves the best ACC for most types of corruptions. The mean ACC of our ASPECTS is 74.28%, which is +1.51% higher than the runner-up (*i.e.*, L2D).

Comparison on Medical Datasets. We further compare the proposed ASPECTS and the competitive single-DG approach (L2D) on MIDOG and private multicentre colposcopic image datasets. Due to the smaller amount of medical data, a shallow network [12] is adopted as backbone. Note that we re-implement L2D using the shallow backbone and report the results in this section for the fair comparison. The single domain generalization accuracies yielded by

Table 2. The ACC (%) yielded by different approaches on MIDOG [1] under the single domain generalization setting.

Source domain	S1		S2		S3		Mean
Target domain	S2	S3	S1	S3	S1	S2	
Baseline	60.50	55.09	58.55	56.89	56.00	60.32	57.89
L2D [14]	65.23	58.68	61.19	57.51	59.74	63.90	61.04
Ours w/o $\mathcal{A}_c^r$	63.11	57.57	60.34	57.13	58.04	62.14	59.72
Ours w/o $\mathcal{A}_c^s$	62.99	57.51	61.62	58.37	57.70	61.10	59.88
ASPECTS	**65.66**	**60.05**	**62.64**	**60.42**	**62.57**	**65.78**	**62.85**

Table 3. Single domain generalization accuracy (%) on the private colposcopic image dataset. Centre #1 is taken as the source domain and the other centres are evaluated as target domains.

	Centre #2	Centre #3	Centre #4	Centre #5	Centre #6	Mean
Baseline	70.71	55.99	55.67	53.06	60.69	59.22
L2D [14]	71.23	58.17	57.59	55.75	62.67	61.08
ASPECTS	**72.06**	**60.11**	**61.56**	**57.14**	**63.46**	**62.87**

different approaches on MIDOG and colposcopic image datasets are presented in Table 2 and Table 3, respectively.

For MIDOG, we form three settings by using each scanner as the source domain. It can be observed that our ASPECTS consistently surpasses the state-of-the-art L2D across different scenarios. Concretely, the mean ACC of the proposed ASPECTS is +1.81% higher than L2D. Similar trend is observed on the multicentre colposcopic image dataset. Our ASPECTS outperforms the state-of-the-art L2D by a large margin of +1.79% (mean ACC). It is worthwhile to mention that, compared to L2D, our ASPECTS can be easily incorporated into existing approaches without revision of network architecture.[5]

Ablation Study. We conduct an ablation study on MIDOG to evaluate the contribution of different randomization operations of our ASPECTS and present the results in Table 2. It can be observed that the mean ACC of our ASPECTS degrades to around 59% by removing either operation. Such a result demonstrates using both randomization operations can further diversify the adversarial samples and accordingly boost the single-DG accuracy.

4 Conclusion

In this paper, we proposed an intuitive spontaneous Amplitude SPECTrum diverSification (ASPECTS) approach for single domain generalization. Particu-

---

[5] Note that L2D needs to integrate an extra style-complement module into the framework for sample diversification.

larly, the proposed ASPECTS first transformed the image into frequency domain using the Fourier transform, and then spontaneously yielded diverse adversarial samples by editing the amplitude spectrum. The proposed ASPECTS approach was evaluated on both publicly available and private multi-domain datasets. The experimental results showed that our ASPECTS significantly outperformed the state-of-the-art single-DG approaches. Furthermore, compared to the existing single-DG frameworks, our method is much easier to implement (*i.e.,* without training of extra network modules).

References

1. Aubreville, M., Bertram, C.A., Donovan, T.A., Marzahl, C., Maier, A., Klopfleisch, R.: A completely annotated whole slide image dataset of canine breast cancer to aid human breast cancer research. Sci. Data **7**(1), 1–10 (2020)
2. Bian, C., et al.: Uncertainty-aware domain alignment for anatomical structure segmentation. Med. Image Anal. **64**, 101732 (2020)
3. Du, Y., et al.: Learning to learn with variational information bottleneck for domain generalization. In: Vedaldi, A., Bischof, H., Brox, T., Frahm, J.-M. (eds.) ECCV 2020. LNCS, vol. 12355, pp. 200–216. Springer, Cham (2020). https://doi.org/10.1007/978-3-030-58607-2_12
4. Hansen, B.C., Hess, R.F.: Structural sparseness and spatial phase alignment in natural scenes. J. Opt. Soc. Am. A **24**(7), 1873–1885 (2007)
5. Hendrycks, D., Dietterich, T.: Benchmarking neural network robustness to common corruptions and perturbations. arXiv preprint arXiv:1903.12261 (2009)
6. Huang, Z., Wang, H., Xing, E.P., Huang, D.: Self-challenging improves cross-domain generalization. In: Vedaldi, A., Bischof, H., Brox, T., Frahm, J.-M. (eds.) ECCV 2020. LNCS, vol. 12347, pp. 124–140. Springer, Cham (2020). https://doi.org/10.1007/978-3-030-58536-5_8
7. Krizhevsky, A., Hinton, G., et al.: Learning multiple layers of features from tiny images (2009)
8. Motiian, S., Piccirilli, M., Adjeroh, D.A., Doretto, G.: Unified deep supervised domain adaptation and generalization. In: IEEE International Conference on Computer Vision (2017)
9. Oppenheim, A., Lim, J.: The importance of phase in signals. Proc. IEEE **69**(5), 529–541 (1981)
10. Piotrowski, L.N., Campbell, F.W.: A demonstration of the visual importance and flexibility of spatial-frequency amplitude and phase. Perception **11**(3), 337–346 (1982)
11. Qiao, F., Zhao, L., Peng, X.: Learning to learn single domain generalization. In: IEEE Conference on Computer Vision and Pattern Recognition (2020)
12. Simon, C., Koniusz, P., Nock, R., Harandi, M.: Adaptive subspaces for few-shot learning. In: IEEE Conference on Computer Vision and Pattern Recognition (2020)
13. Volpi, R., Namkoong, H., Sener, O., Duchi, J.C., Murino, V., Savarese, S.: Generalizing to unseen domains via adversarial data augmentation. In: Advances in Neural Information Processing Systems, vol. 31 (2018)
14. Wang, Z., Luo, Y., Qiu, R., Huang, Z., Baktashmotlagh, M.: Learning to diversify for single domain generalization. In: IEEE International Conference on Computer Vision (2021)

15. Xie, X., Chen, J., Li, Y., Shen, L., Ma, K., Zheng, Y.: MI^{2}GAN: generative adversarial network for medical image domain adaptation using mutual information constraint. In: Martel, A.L., et al. (eds.) MICCAI 2020. LNCS, vol. 12262, pp. 516–525. Springer, Cham (2020). https://doi.org/10.1007/978-3-030-59713-9_50
16. Xu, Q., Zhang, R., Zhang, Y., Wang, Y., Tian, Q.: A Fourier-based framework for domain generalization. In: IEEE Conference on Computer Vision and Pattern Recognition (2021)
17. Xu, X., Zhou, X., Venkatesan, R., Swaminathan, G., Majumder, O.: d-SNE: domain adaptation using stochastic neighborhood embedding. In: IEEE Conference on Computer Vision and Pattern Recognition (2019)
18. Xue, Y., Feng, S., Zhang, Y., Zhang, X., Wang, Y.: Dual-task self-supervision for cross-modality domain adaptation. In: Martel, A.L., et al. (eds.) MICCAI 2020. LNCS, vol. 12261, pp. 408–417. Springer, Cham (2020). https://doi.org/10.1007/978-3-030-59710-8_40
19. Yang, Y., Soatto, S.: FDA: Fourier domain adaptation for semantic segmentation. In: IEEE Conference on Computer Vision and Pattern Recognition (2020)
20. Zagoruyko, S., Komodakis, N.: Wide residual networks. arXiv preprint arXiv:1605.07146 (2017)
21. Zhang, T., et al.: Noise adaptation generative adversarial network for medical image analysis. IEEE Trans. Med. Imaging 39(4), 1149–1159 (2020)
22. Zhao, L., Liu, T., Peng, X., Metaxas, D.: Maximum-entropy adversarial data augmentation for improved generalization and robustness. Adv. Neural. Inf. Process. Syst. 33, 14435–14447 (2020)
23. Zhou, K., Yang, Y., Hospedales, T., Xiang, T.: Learning to generate novel domains for domain generalization. In: Vedaldi, A., Bischof, H., Brox, T., Frahm, J.-M. (eds.) ECCV 2020. LNCS, vol. 12361, pp. 561–578. Springer, Cham (2020). https://doi.org/10.1007/978-3-030-58517-4_33

Triple-View Feature Learning for Medical Image Segmentation

Ziyang Wang$^{(\boxtimes)}$ and Irina Voiculescu

Department of Computer Science, University of Oxford, Oxford, UK
ziyang.wang@cs.ox.ac.uk

Abstract. Deep learning models, e.g. supervised Encoder-Decoder style networks, exhibit promising performance in medical image segmentation, but come with a high labelling cost. We propose TriSegNet, a semi-supervised semantic segmentation framework. It uses *triple-view* feature learning on a limited amount of labelled data and a large amount of unlabeled data. The triple-view architecture consists of three pixel-level classifiers and a low-level shared-weight learning module. The model is first initialized with labelled data. Label processing, including data perturbation, confidence label voting and unconfident label detection for annotation, enables the model to train on labelled and unlabeled data simultaneously. The confidence of each model gets improved through the other two views of the feature learning. This process is repeated until each model reaches the same confidence level as its counterparts. This strategy enables triple-view learning of generic medical image datasets. Bespoke overlap-based and boundary-based loss functions are tailored to the different stages of the training. The segmentation results are evaluated on four publicly available benchmark datasets including Ultrasound, CT, MRI, and Histology images. Repeated experiments demonstrate the effectiveness of the proposed network compared against other semi-supervised algorithms, across a large set of evaluation measures.

1 Introduction

The promising performance of deep learning for medical imaging relies not only on network architecture engineering, but also on the availability of sufficient high-quality manually annotated data, which is hard to come by. Co-training, and self-training are two widely studied approaches in semi-supervised learning.

Self-training first initializes a model with labelled data. Then the model generates pseudo masks for unlabelled data. A condition is set for the selection of pseudo masks, and the model is retrained by expanding its training data [29].

Co-training is normally used to train two separate models with two views which benefit each other [3] by expanding the size of the training data. Deep co-training was first proposed by [18] pointing out the challenge of 'collapsed neural networks': training two models on the same dataset cannot enable multi-view feature learning because the two models will necessarily end up similar.

X. Xu et al. (Eds.): REMIA 2022, LNCS 13543, pp. 42–54, 2022.
https://doi.org/10.1007/978-3-031-16876-5_5

Output smearing, diversity augmentation, and dropout for pseudo label editing were designed to mitigate that effect [5].

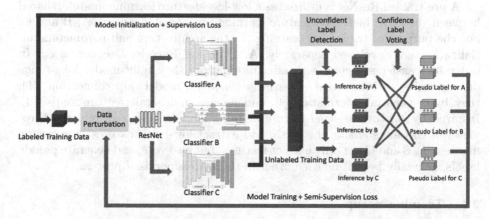

Fig. 1. The architecture of TriSegNet framework

2 Methodology

The central idea in our method is that several (three in our case) different views of the data and their associated learned parameters are developed in separate models simultaneously. This gives each model a chance to complement the others in what they contribute to the learning process. Moreover, they do not each process the same dataset: rather, they take carefully crafted disjoint parts of the data and learn what they can from each of those subsets.

A multi-view co-training semi-supervised learning method for classification is also proposed in [5], but for a classification task, not for semantic segmentation. Detailed mask prediction requires an entirely novel technique [7,24]. Our pseudo-labels are generated afresh at intermediate steps selecting from amongst the output of two individual CNN components in order to train the third one. Our confidence estimation is different from the uncertainty-aware scheme [25,26]: the triple framework decides which pseudo-labels to propagate further through selecting those in which the individual component models have had high confidence and have 'voted' for. This also has the effect of increasing the overall confidence of the framework in a way that we specifically show how to measure. Pseudo-labels with too low a confidence level are not used in the following step. How low that level of confidence depends on the stage of the training: the further into the training process, the more confident the framework needs to become. Thus the number of images available for training gets increased gradually.

The architecture of our **Tri**ple-view feature learning for medical image semantic **Seg**mentation **Net**work (TriSegNet) is illustrated in Fig. 1. The label editing including unconfident label detection and confidence label voting based on a confidence estimate improves the feature expression of un-annotated data. Each of the three views of the feature learning makes use of random data perturbation for regularization.

A pre-trained ResNet is utilized as a low-level feature learning module, shared between the three high-level feature learning pixel-level classifiers A, B and C. For the purpose of triple-view learning [7], the architecture and parameters initialization are developed separately. A, B, C are Encoder-Decoder-based. In order to transfer sufficient semantic information, they fully model long-range dependencies, variation size of feature expression, model skip connection [19], they bypass spatial information [4], and process multi-scale feature maps [14]. Inspired by [9], the low-level feature learning module is shared, and the three views of classifiers enable the ResNet to extract low-level features in a generic manner. A, B and C not only extract features, but also vote, and generate pseudo labels, generally benefiting each other in the semi-supervised process.

2.1   Training Setup

We denote by $\mathcal{L}, \mathcal{U}, \mathcal{T}$ a small labelled dataset, a large size of unlabelled dataset, and a dataset for testing. Each batch of labeled data is $(x, y_{gt}) \in \mathcal{L}$, $(x, y_{gt}) \in \mathcal{T}$; batches of only raw data are $(x) \in \mathcal{U}$; y_{pred}, y_{pseudo} is the dense map generated by different views of TriSeg-Net for prediction. We split the training process into three stages with an inference stage. **Stage 1** initializes the three views of classifiers $f_n, n = 1, 2, 3$ with labeled dataset $\mathcal{L}$, repeatedly, as shown in Fig. 2(d), with data perturbation as per Fig. 2(a). To properly initialize the three classifiers with unbalanced data, overlap loss is used. The confidence weight during the training process is estimated and recorded as $\alpha_n, n = 1, 2, 3$ until inference is complete. Each model estimates its confidence of the labelled data by on randomly selected pseudo labels, also compared against the

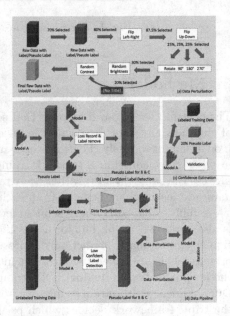

Fig. 2. Data pipeline and label processing stages.

other two models as sketched in Fig. 2(c). **Stage 2** learns from the generated pseudo labels in an iterative manner. Unlabeled data $(x) \in \mathcal{U}$ are used by f_n as (x, y_{n_pred}) pairs. Any data corresponding to low confidence labels gets removed. A fresh vote from another model f_n generates pseudo label $(x, y_{n\_pseudo}) = \alpha_{n-1} \times f_{n-1}(x) + \alpha_{n+1} \times f_{n+1}(x)$ to train the rest of the model. The loss function at this stage is mixed overlap- and boundary-based loss. **Stage 3** is to train additionally the lowest confident classifier with $\mathcal{L}, \mathcal{U}$. The learning rate for all training stages is set to 2×10^{-4}, with an Adam optimizer. The training epoch is set to 150 in Stage 1, 100 in Stage 2, and 150 or early stopped until the least confident classifier reaches the same confidence as other classifiers in Stage 3. The batch size is set to 16. **Inference** is to predict jointly on an unseen image $(x) \in \mathcal{T}$ to $y_{pred} = \sum_{n=1}^{3} \alpha_n \times f_n(x)$.

2.2   Label Processing

To encourage meaningful differences among views for co-training, it is essential to pin down each classifier's architecture, as well as its label editing. In TriSegNet we propose three label editing approaches: Data perturbation, low confidence label detection, and Confidence label voting.

Data Perturbation. Mean Teacher [20] uses perturbation to assess the consistency of the same image under different disturbances. This is extended in Dual Student to pixel-wise tasks in guided collaborative training [13]. Naive-student [6] uses perturbation for pseudo labels in an iterative manner to train the student network. To effect differences between the three views, TriSegNet also uses perturbation in an iterative manner, in each training epoch and separately for each of the views, as detailed in Fig. 2. From the input data, 70% is selected, then 80% of this is processed by left-right and up-down flips, and 25% has 90°, 180°, 270° rotations applied. Random brightness and contrast changes are applied to 20% and 30% of the data respectively. Data perturbation is used both on labelled data and on the pseudo labels predicted from each classifier.

Low Confidence Label Detection. A badly performing view may negatively influence the whole framework in that it predicts pseudo labels for the other two views. Uncertainty estimation might be tackled with agreement-based entropy-maps or using pseudo labels for training, or computing uncertainty-weighted with a Bayesian deep network by adding dropout layers [7,25,26]. Instead, we mark any unreliable pseudo labels as noisy [11,23], thus temporarily removing low confidence labels from one view with the help of the other two views. Retaining only high confidence pseudo labels boosts the overall performance. A simple adaptive denoising learning strategy is to calculate the overlap-based difference between each prediction in different views and record it for each pseudo label in each training epoch. The higher the label difference, the higher the probability of it not being accepted. During each training epoch with prediction label (x, y_{pred}), our strategy detects and removes specific number of the high difference labels (x, y_{pseudo}) raised by the other two views. More low confidence labels get detected at the beginning of the training iteration, and fewer towards the end., because the training process evolves from underfitting to overfitting. The number $N(t)$ of removed labels is

$$N(t) = \begin{cases} 0.05(1-\zeta)y, & 0 < t < 0.01(1-\zeta)x \\ \frac{-y}{x}t + 0.06(1-\zeta)y, & 0.01(1-\zeta)x \le t \& t \le 0.05(1-\zeta)x \\ 0.01(1-\zeta)y, & 0.05(1-\zeta)x < t \le x \end{cases} \quad (1)$$

where t is the current training iteration, ζ is the difference/disagreement level, x is the total number of training iterations, and y is the total number of y_{pred}.

Confidence Label Voting. The uncertainty of the pseudo labels can sabotage expanding the training data, potentially influencing the whole framework performance. Luo [17] studied pyramid prediction network and uncertainty rectified pyramid consistency. Yu [30] proposed a Monte Carlo Dropout to generate an uncertainty map in student-teacher networks. Xia [26] proposed uncertainty weighted label fusion. Unlike the student-teacher network or single encoder-decoder networks, or directly calculating the average maximum posterior probability of another two views, Tri-net [5] proposes a direct confidence estimate. In our algorithm, labelled training data and 20% of un-perturbed pseudo label data is considered as a validation set for each view to obtain confidence weights; thus two views jointly generate pseudo labels for the last view using confidence voting together after low confidence label detection for cross pseudo supervision [7].

2.3   Loss Function

The weight of pseudo-label-based semi-supervision loss relative to labeled-based supervised loss increases gradually during training, as the model becomes progressively more confident in generating and using pseudo labels [7,15,20]. A low to high confidence strategy has been explored in uncertainty-aware schemes [30]. TriSegNet enables coarse-to-fine model training using gradually more precise pseudo labels: in Stage 1 an overlap-based loss is used (Eq. 2), whereas Stages 2 and 3 rely on a mixed overlap- and boundary-based loss (Eq. 3). Overlap-based loss is more robust when the datasets are imbalanced (e.g. fewer True pixels). Once the pseudo labels from each view become dependable, the dual loss is triggered, enabling the three views to segment more precisely [8].

$$Loss_{stage1} = \left(1 - \frac{TP + 10^{-6}}{TP + \alpha FN + \beta FP + 10^{-6}}\right)^{\gamma} \qquad (2)$$

$$Loss_{stage2\&3} = \underbrace{\sum_{i,j=1}^{256} \sqrt{\| \nabla P_{x_{i,j}} + \nabla P_{y_{i,j}} + 10^{-6}\|}}_{Loss_{Boundary}} +$$

$$\underbrace{\| \sum_{i,j=1}^{256} P_{i,j}(1 - G_{i,j})^2 \| + \| \sum_{i,j=1}^{256} (1 - P_{i,j})G_{i,j}^2 \|}_{Loss_{Overlap}} \qquad (3)$$

The ground truth, and pseudo label are denoted as $G, P \in [0,1]^{256 \times 256}$, where 1 and 0 denote the region of interest or the background on a 256×256 image. Constants α, β and γ control the non-linearity of the loss [16].

3   Experiments and Results

3.1   Datasets and Experimental Setup

Our experiments have been carried out on four public benchmark datasets: (1) The Ultrasound Nerve Segmentation Kaggle Challenge [12] Identifying nerve structures in ultrasound images is critical to inserting a patient's pain management catheter. We use 5,635 images of size 580×420. (2) The MRI Cardiac Segmentation is from the Automated Cardiac Diagnosis MICCAI Challenge 2017 [2]. We use 1,203 images of size 232×256, from 150 patients. (3) The Histology Nuclei Segmentation is a Pan-Cancer histology dataset from the University of Warwick [10]. We use 7,901 images of size 256×256. (4) The CT Spine set includes 10 CTs from a CSI 2014 Segmentation Challenge [27], covering the entire thoracic and lumbar spine. We use 5,602 images of size 512×512.

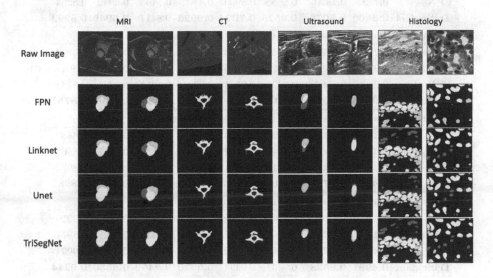

Fig. 3. Sample qualitative results; Two images are selected from each test set where the first row illustrates the raw images. The rest of them illustrate the MS against GT where yellow, green, red, and black represent TP, FN, FP and TN at the pixel level

Ultrasound, MRI and Histology images have been resized to 256×256, and CTs to 512×512. All four are pre-processed with data perturbation. The data has been split into labelled training data, test data and unlabeled raw training data. The test data is always 10% of the set, selected randomly for each run. The training data is the remainder of the dataset; for separate experiments, 2%, 5%, 10% or 20% of this is available labelled, and the rest is available raw. The validation data is selected as a separate random 20% sample of the training set (both labelled and not), and is never seen by the training process.

We used Python 3.8.8, Tensorflow 2.6.0 [1] and CUDA 11.3, on four Nvidia GeForce RTX3090 GPUs. The runtimes averaged 2–3.5 h on the MRI data, and

6–8 h on the Ultrasound, CT and Histology data, including the data transfer, three training stages, inference and evaluation. Semi-supervised learning for medical image segmentation[1], an online collection of implementations has been used in the baseline testing models and additional Dropout.

Table 1. Evaluation results on direct comparison between TriSegNet and existing fully-supervised algorithms

	Ultrasound nerve		CT spine		MRI cardiac		Histology nuclei	
	IOU	Sen	IOU	Sen	IOU	Sen	IOU	Sen
Experiments under the assumption of **2%** *data as labeled data*								
UNet	0.1628	0.2020	0.8657	0.9210	0.3888	0.8351	0.6574	0.7814
Linknet	0.0919	0.1280	0.8438	0.8962	0.1498	**0.9329**	0.6905	0.8219
FPN	0.1227	0.1320	0.8653	0.8990	0.4802	0.5143	0.6942	0.8284
TriSegNet	**0.2800**	**0.3678**	**0.9526**	**0.7024**	**0.9923**	0.8411	**0.6946**	**0.8293**
Experiments under the assumption of **5%** *data as labeled data*								
UNet	0.2762	0.3234	0.9207	0.9576	0.6805	0.8053	0.7075	0.5953
Linknet	0.2505	0.2885	0.9020	0.9519	0.6762	0.7988	0.7552	0.8645
FPN	0.2703	0.3093	0.9221	0.9521	0.7721	0.8351	0.7031	0.8333
TriSegNet	**0.3765**	**0.5090**	**0.9385**	**0.9660**	**0.8094**	**0.8880**	**0.7691**	**0.8757**
Experiments under the assumption of **10%** *data as labeled data*								
UNet	0.3554	0.4090	0.9320	0.9660	0.8492	**0.9253**	0.8012	0.8880
Linknet	0.3464	0.3991	0.9247	0.9527	0.7832	0.8641	0.7957	0.8862
FPN	0.2416	0.4866	0.8316	0.9721	0.8078	0.8591	0.8034	0.8973
TriSegNet	**0.4260**	**0.5789**	**0.9463**	**0.9714**	**0.8545**	0.9159	**0.8114**	**0.8981**
Experiments under the assumption of **20%** *data as labeled data*								
UNet	0.4352	0.5254	**0.9447**	**0.9699**	0.8984	0.9448	0.8104	0.9019
Linknet	0.4333	0.5237	0.9295	0.9678	0.8712	0.9258	0.8027	0.8971
FPN	0.3956	0.5953	0.7605	0.8920	0.8857	0.9307	0.8176	0.9094
TriSegNet	**0.4981**	**0.6528**	0.9337	0.9494	**0.9020**	**0.9459**	**0.8530**	**0.9244**

3.2   Evaluation and Results

Performance has been assessed using a wide range of evaluation metrics. These include the frequently reported similarity measures: Dice, IOU, accuracy, precision, sensitivity, specificity, as well as difference measures: relative volume difference (RVD), Hausdorff distance (HD), average symmetric surface distance (ASSD). To penalise mislabelled areas and avoid overly inflated segmentation scores, we also evaluate the boundary match between the machine segmentation (MS) and the Ground Truth (GT), using the Directed Boundary Dice relative to GT (DBD_G) and to MS (DBD_M) and Symmetric Boundary Dice (SBD) [28].

---

[1] https://github.com/HiLab-git/SSL4MIS.

Table 2. Direct comparison of TriSegNet with other algorithms, on the MRI test set

Model	Dice	Acc	Pre	Rec/Sen	Spe	RVD	HD	ASSD	DBD$_G$	DBD$_M$	SBD
[20]	0.895	0.992	0.909	0.881	0.996	0.226	21.876	4.077	0.561	0.649	0.599
[22]	0.881	0.991	0.918	0.847	0.997	0.273	18.335	3.954	0.543	**0.651**	0.589
[31]	0.878	0.990	0.858	0.899	0.994	0.332	24.235	5.046	0.577	0.564	0.559
[30]	0.890	0.991	0.903	0.878	0.996	0.244	22.851	4.669	0.550	0.636	0.585
[21]	0.899	0.992	0.909	0.889	0.996	**0.205**	28.388	4.773	0.582	0.639	0.605
TriSegNet	**0.932**	**0.995**	**0.934**	**0.930**	**0.997**	0.208	**7.831**	**2.075**	**0.712**	0.611	**0.657**

Table 3. Ablation studies on contributions of architecture and modules

Label process	Dual loss design	Classifier A	Classifier B	Classifier C	IOU
		✓ × 2	✓		0.8724
			✓ × 2	✓	0.8739
		✓		✓ × 2	0.8641
✓		✓ × 3			0.8666
	✓	✓ × 3			0.8579
			✓ × 3		0.8598
✓			✓ × 3		0.8605
				✓ × 3	0.8619
✓				✓ × 3	0.8739
✓		✓	✓	✓	0.8787
	✓	✓	✓	✓	0.8841
✓	✓	✓	✓	✓	0.9020

Experiments first compare TriSegNet with fully-supervised baseline methods like UNet [19], LinkNet [4] and FPN [14]. Table 1 reports the quantitative results for each dataset, using 2%–20% of labeled data. The examples in Fig. 3 illustrate these comparisons qualitatively.

To illustrate a wider range of evaluation measures with semi-supervised algorithms, there is only room to report on one dataset. The MRI Cardiac data has been chosen for this purpose. Table 2 documents the performance of TriSegNet against Tarvainen [20], Vu [22], Zhang [31], Yu [30], Verma [21] with UNet as backbone, showing that it outperforms previous methods under most of the considered metrics.

In order to assess the contribution of each of the components, specifically focused ablation experiments have been designed. They illustrate the essential role of models A, B and C being different by considering, instead of the three, two copies of one of them ($A\times2$, $A\times3$, etc.). Table 3 illustrates that the IOU metric is negatively influenced by such choices, performing best when each of A, B and C is present in its own right.

4   Conclusion

Four medical datasets with different labelled/unlabelled assumptions have been used in the experiments. A series of experiments are designed including the comparison between TriSegNet and fully-supervised learning algorithms, as well as its comparison with other semi-supervised learning algorithms. Ablation studies justify the design decisions. Although a common Dice-based loss function is used for the initial stages of the training process, a bespoke boundary-overlap-based loss is used in the more advanced stages. This increases the confidence of the model in its predictions and hence the reliability of the pseudo labels it generates. Overall, TriSegNet demonstrates promising performance in most evaluation metrics, showing great potential in semi-supervised learning for general medical image segmentation.

A Algorithm of TriSegNet

The training of TriSegNet consists of four stages which is briefly illustrated in Algorithm 1. The code of TriSegNet will be publicly available[2].

B The CNN Architecture of Multi-view Learning

To properly encourage the differences of the three views of feature learning on dense prediction, not only the data feed and initialization of parameters, but three different advanced CNN are proposed in TriSegNet. We utilize three different techniques for CNN i.e. skip connection, efficiently passing feature information through residual learning, and multi-scale feature learning. The parameters of three classifiers are briefly illustrated in Table 4 and the source code has been released online[3].

C Evaluation Methods, Qualitative, and Quantitative Results

Table 2 reports the TriSegNet performance direct comparison with other algorithms with several strict and novel quantitative evaluation metrics to which the boundaries of the machine segmentation(MS) match those of the ground truth(GT), using the Directed Boundary Dice relative to GT (DBD_G), Directed Boundary Dice relative to MS (DBD_M) and Symmetric Boundary Dice (SBD).

In a von Neumann neighbourhood N_x of each pixel x on the boundary ∂G of the ground truth,

$$DBD_G = DBD(G, M) = \frac{\sum\limits_{x \in \partial G} \mathrm{Dice}(N_x)}{|\partial G|} \quad (4)$$

---

[2] https://github.com/ziyangwang007/CV-SSL-MIS.

[3] https://github.com/qubvel/segmentation_models/tree/master/segmentation_models.

Algorithm 1: Training Stage of TriSegNet for Medical Image Segmentation

---

Input: A batch of (x, y) from labeled dataset $\mathcal{L}$, unlabeled dataset $\mathcal{U}$, or test dataset $\mathcal{T}$. DA, $LCLE$, and CLV are label processing approaches Data Augmentation, Low Confidence Label Editing, and Confident Label Voting, respectively.

Output: Three trained high-level feature learning classifiers. $f_n, n = 1, 2, 3$

Stage one: Initialization

$\theta_1, \theta_2, \theta_3 \leftarrow$ initial parameters of classifiers f_1, f_2, f_3, and the loss function $L_{Supervision}$.

while $n \leftarrow$ [1, 2, 3] (3 classifiers) **do**
    (x, y_{gt}) sampled from $DA(\mathcal{L})$ with augmentation;
    Generate prediction $y_{pred} = f_n(x)$;
    Calculate loss $L_{Supervision}$ with $y_{pred} = y_{gt}$;
    Update $\theta_n \leftarrow \theta_n - \Delta L$;
end

Stage two: Classifiers Training with Pseudo Label Processing

$\alpha_1, \alpha_2, \alpha_3 \leftarrow$ initial confidence weight of classifiers f_1, f_2, f_3 ;

while $n \leftarrow$ [1, 2, 3], $i \leftarrow$ [1...5] (5 Iterations) **do**
    x sampled from $DA(\mathcal{U})$ with augmentation ;
    Generate pseudo label for Classifier f_n
    $y_{n\_pseudo} = CLV(LCLE(f_{n-1}(x)), LCLE(f_{n+1}(x)))$;
    Calculate loss $L_{SemiSupervision}$ with $y_{pred} = y_{n\_pseudo}$;
    Update $\theta_n \leftarrow \theta_n - \Delta L$;
    Update $\alpha_n \leftarrow$ with L by evaluation dataset ;
end

Stage three. One low confidence Classifier Training

while $n \leftarrow$ [1, 2, 3], $i \leftarrow$ [1...5] **do**
    If Network f_n is with the lowest α_n **Then** (x, y_{gt}) sampled from $DA(\mathcal{L})$;
    (x, y_{n_pseudo}) sampled from $DA(\mathcal{U})$;
    Generate pseudo label for Classifer f_n
    $y_{n\_pseudo} = CLV(LCLE(f_{n-1}(x)), LCLE(f_{n+1}(x)))$;
    Calculate loss L with $y_{pred} = y_{n\_pseudo}$;
    Update $\theta_n \leftarrow \theta_n - \Delta L_{SemiSupervision}$;
    Update $\alpha_n \leftarrow$ with L by evaluation dataset ;
end

Table 4. The computation cost information of three classifier

Model	Total params	Trainable params	Non-trainable params
Classifier A	32,561,120	32,513,562	47,558
Classifier B	20,323,985	20,317,169	47,558
Classifier C	17,594,453	17,592,149	2,304

52   Z. Wang and I. Voiculescu

$$DBD_M = DBD(M,G) = \frac{\sum\limits_{x \in \partial M} \text{Dice}(N_Y)}{|\partial M|} \qquad (5)$$

$$SBD = \frac{\sum\limits_{x \in \partial G} DSC(N_x) + \sum\limits_{y \in \partial M} DSC(N_y)}{|\partial G| + |\partial M|} \qquad (6)$$

where Dice is $Dice(N_x) = \frac{2|G(N_x) \cap M(N_y)|}{|G(N_x)| + |M(N_y)|}$. The symmetric average is being brought down by DBD_G when the latter features isolated areas of false negative labels. These measures penalise mislabelled areas in the machine segmentation.

Some of example qualitative results on MRI Cardiac test set are briefly sketched in Fig. 4. Eight images are selected from MRI test set where the first row illustrates raw images. The rest of them illustrate the MS by each semi-supervised algorithm against GT where yellow, green, red, and black represent true positive, false negative, false positive and true negative at pixel level. The proposed method shows fewer false positive and false negative pixels, and significantly low HD as well, because the TriSegNet is beneficial with different views of high-level pixel-level classifier and proposed mixed boundary- and overlap-based loss function.

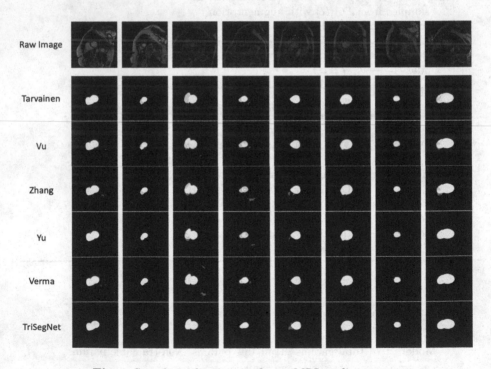

Fig. 4. Sample qualitative results on MRI cardiac test set

References

1. Abadi, M., et al.: TensorFlow: large-scale machine learning on heterogeneous systems (2015). www.tensorflow.org/
2. Bernard, O., et al.: Deep learning techniques for automatic MRI cardiac multi-structures segmentation and diagnosis: is the problem solved? IEEE Trans. Med. Imaging **37**(11), 2514–2525 (2018)
3. Blum, A., Mitchell, T.: Combining labeled and unlabeled data with co-training. In: Proceedings of the Eleventh Annual Conference on Computational Learning Theory, pp. 92–100 (1998)
4. Chaurasia, A., Culurciello, E.: Linknet: exploiting encoder representations for efficient semantic segmentation. In: 2017 IEEE Visual Communications and Image Processing, pp. 1–4. IEEE (2017)
5. Chen, D.D., et al.: Tri-net for semi-supervised deep learning. In: International Joint Conferences on Artificial Intelligence (2018)
6. Chen, L.-C., et al.: Naive-student: leveraging semi-supervised learning in video sequences for urban scene segmentation. In: Vedaldi, A., Bischof, H., Brox, T., Frahm, J.-M. (eds.) ECCV 2020. LNCS, vol. 12354, pp. 695–714. Springer, Cham (2020). https://doi.org/10.1007/978-3-030-58545-7_40
7. Chen, X., et al.: Semi-supervised semantic segmentation with cross pseudo supervision. In: Proceedings of the IEEE/CVF Conference on Computer Vision and Pattern Recognition, pp. 2613–2622 (2021)
8. Chen, X., et al.: Learning active contour models for medical image segmentation. In: Proceedings of the IEEE/CVF Conference on Computer Vision and Pattern Recognition, pp. 11632–11640 (2019)
9. Donahue, J., et al.: DeCAF: a deep convolutional activation feature for generic visual recognition. In: International Conference on Machine Learning, pp. 647–655. PMLR (2014)
10. Gamper, J., Alemi Koohbanani, N., Benet, K., Khuram, A., Rajpoot, N.: PanNuke: an open pan-cancer histology dataset for nuclei instance segmentation and classification. In: Reyes-Aldasoro, C.C., Janowczyk, A., Veta, M., Bankhead, P., Sirinukunwattana, K. (eds.) ECDP 2019. LNCS, vol. 11435, pp. 11–19. Springer, Cham (2019). https://doi.org/10.1007/978-3-030-23937-4_2
11. Huang, J., et al.: O2u-net: a simple noisy label detection approach for deep neural networks. In: Proceedings of the IEEE International Conference on Computer Vision, pp. 3326–3334 (2019)
12. Kaggle: Ultrasound nerve segmentation. www.kaggle.com/c/ultrasound-nerve-segmentation
13. Ke, Z., Qiu, D., Li, K., Yan, Q., Lau, R.W.H.: Guided collaborative training for pixel-wise semi-supervised learning. In: Vedaldi, A., Bischof, H., Brox, T., Frahm, J.-M. (eds.) ECCV 2020. LNCS, vol. 12358, pp. 429–445. Springer, Cham (2020). https://doi.org/10.1007/978-3-030-58601-0_26
14. Kim, S.W., et al.: Parallel feature pyramid network for object detection. In: Proceedings of the European Conference on Computer Vision, pp. 234–250 (2018)
15. Laine, S., Aila, T.: Temporal ensembling for semi-supervised learning. arXiv preprint arXiv:1610.02242 (2016)
16. Lin, T.Y., Goyal, P., Girshick, R., He, K., Dollár, P.: Focal loss for dense object detection. In: Proceedings of the IEEE International Conference on Computer Vision, pp. 2980–2988 (2017)

17. Luo, X., et al.: Efficient semi-supervised gross target volume of nasopharyngeal carcinoma segmentation via uncertainty rectified pyramid consistency. In: de Bruijne, M., et al. (eds.) MICCAI 2021. LNCS, vol. 12902, pp. 318–329. Springer, Cham (2021). https://doi.org/10.1007/978-3-030-87196-3_30

18. Qiao, S., et al.: Deep co-training for semi-supervised image recognition. In: Proceedings of the European Conference on Computer Vision, pp. 135–152 (2018)

19. Ronneberger, O., Fischer, P., Brox, T.: U-Net: convolutional networks for biomedical image segmentation. In: Navab, N., Hornegger, J., Wells, W.M., Frangi, A.F. (eds.) MICCAI 2015. LNCS, vol. 9351, pp. 234–241. Springer, Cham (2015). https://doi.org/10.1007/978-3-319-24574-4_28

20. Tarvainen, A., Valpola, H.: Mean teachers are better role models: Weight-averaged consistency targets improve semi-supervised deep learning results. In: Proceedings of the 31st International Conference on Neural Information Processing Systems, pp. 1195–1204 (2017)

21. Verma, V., et al.: Interpolation consistency training for semi-supervised learning. In: International Joint Conference on Artificial Intelligence, pp. 3635–3641 (2019)

22. Vu, T.H., et al.: Advent: adversarial entropy minimization for domain adaptation in semantic segmentation. In: Proceedings of the IEEE/CVF Conference on Computer Vision and Pattern Recognition, pp. 2517–2526 (2019)

23. Wang, Z., Zhang, Z., Voiculescu, I.: RAR-U-Net: a residual encoder to attention decoder by residual connections framework for spine segmentation under noisy labels. In: Proceedings of the IEEE International Conference on Image Processing. IEEE (2021)

24. Wang, Z., et al.: Computationally-efficient vision transformer for medical image semantic segmentation via dual pseudo-label supervision. In: IEEE International Conference on Image Processing (ICIP) (2022)

25. Wang, Z., et al.: An uncertainty-aware transformer for MRI cardiac semantic segmentation via mean teachers. In: Yang, G., Aviles-Rivero, A., Roberts, M., Schönlieb, C.B., et al. (eds.) Medical Image Understanding and Analysis. Springer, Cham (2022). https://doi.org/10.1007/978-3-031-12053-4_37

26. Xia, Y., et al.: 3D semi-supervised learning with uncertainty-aware multi-view cotraining. In: Proceedings of the IEEE/CVF Winter Conference on Applications of Computer Vision, pp. 3646–3655 (2020)

27. Yao, J., Burns, J.E., Munoz, H., Summers, R.M.: Detection of vertebral body fractures based on cortical shell unwrapping. In: Ayache, N., Delingette, H., Golland, P., Mori, K. (eds.) MICCAI 2012. LNCS, vol. 7512, pp. 509–516. Springer, Heidelberg (2012). https://doi.org/10.1007/978-3-642-33454-2_63

28. Yeghiazaryan, V., Voiculescu, I.D.: Family of boundary overlap metrics for the evaluation of medical image segmentation. SPIE J. Med. Imaging 5(1), 015006 (2018)

29. You, X., et al.: Segmentation of retinal blood vessels using the radial projection and semi-supervised approach. Pattern Recogn. 44(10–11), 2314–2324 (2011)

30. Yu, L., Wang, S., Li, X., Fu, C.-W., Heng, P.-A.: Uncertainty-aware self-ensembling model for semi-supervised 3d left atrium segmentation. In: Shen, D., et al. (eds.) MICCAI 2019. LNCS, vol. 11765, pp. 605–613. Springer, Cham (2019). https://doi.org/10.1007/978-3-030-32245-8_67

31. Zhang, Y., Yang, L., Chen, J., Fredericksen, M., Hughes, D.P., Chen, D.Z.: Deep adversarial networks for biomedical image segmentation utilizing unannotated images. In: Descoteaux, M., Maier-Hein, L., Franz, A., Jannin, P., Collins, D.L., Duchesne, S. (eds.) MICCAI 2017. LNCS, vol. 10435, pp. 408–416. Springer, Cham (2017). https://doi.org/10.1007/978-3-319-66179-7_47

Classification of 4D fMRI Images Using ML, Focusing on Computational and Memory Utilization Efficiency

Nazanin Beheshti[1,2(✉)] and Lennart Johnsson[1]

[1] University of Houston, Houston, TX, USA
[2] Intel Corporation, Santa Clara, CA, USA

Abstract. Resting state functional magnetic resonance images (fMRI) based on BOLD signals are commonly used for classification of patients as having Alzheimer's disease (AD), mild cognitive impairment (MCI) or being cognitive normal (CN). In this research, we represent Resting-State brain activity in Regions-of-Interest (ROI) by subsets of anatomical region voxels formed by segments of a whole brain bounding box Hilbert curve resulting in an average $5\times$ fewer voxels per ROI than the average number of AAL90 region voxels. We represent each 4D ROI data set with a vector that on average reduces a ROI data set from about 55,000 voxel signal values to 100 to 200 aggregated values in our spatial representation and to 15,000–30,000 in our spatial-temporal representation. We show that a Convolutional Neural Network (CNN) with a model size of about 168 kiB and a Transformer model of only 37 kiB yields classification accuracies of 80–90% for AD, MCI, and CN subject binary classification. Training the CNN and Transformer models on a data set of 551 subjects required 188 and 27 s respectively using Pytorch.1.5.0, Python 3.7.7, and CUDA 10.1 on a system with two 10 cores, 2.8 GHz Intel Xeon E5-2670v2 CPUs and one NVIDIA K40 GPU.

Keywords: fMRI · Convolutional Neural Networks · Transformer models

1 Introduction

For Alzheimer's disease (AD) classification brain activity is derived from Blood Oxygen Level-Dependent (BOLD) magnetization captured by functional Magnetic Resonance Imaging (fMRI). Oxygen-rich blood flow is higher in active than non-active brain regions causing active regions to have stronger magnetic properties through the binding of oxygen to hemoglobin and thus stronger MRI signal. Our classification of subjects with respect to having Alzheimer's disease (AD) or Mild Cognitive Impairment (MCI) or being Cognitive Normal (CN) is based on correlation of aggregated voxel BOLD signal intensity magnitude values. The voxel sizes in fMRI for AD classification typically is 2–4 mm [1, 2]. For our classification study subject fMRI data is mapped to the MNI-152 [3] brain template with 3.3 mm resolution. With female and male brain volumes on average being 1130 cm^3 and 1260 cm^3, respectively, the number of MNI-152 voxels for our data sets is in the 31,000–35,000 range. The data sets we used has up to 200

© The Author(s), under exclusive license to Springer Nature Switzerland AG 2022
X. Xu et al. (Eds.): REMIA 2022, LNCS 13543, pp. 55–64, 2022.
https://doi.org/10.1007/978-3-031-16876-5_6

whole-brain time samples each having 48 64 × 64 voxel slices creating a 4D data set of up to 39 M voxel intensity values of which up to 7 M values represent brain voxels (slices extend beyond the brain).

The classification computational complexity in many Machine Learning (ML) methods is reduced by aggregating voxel signals for ROIs then performing classification based on ROI-to-ROI correlations of the voxel aggregates. Accurately defining brain regions, their functions and connections is exceptionally challenging and several parcellation methods exist for the study of structure and function. Anatomical, functional connectivity or hierarchal clustering methods aims to offer meaningful parcellations at different levels of granularity [4–6]. Functional connectivity commonly used for AD classification can be assessed using stimuli, task-based observations, or without stimuli, resting-state (RS) observations [7, 8]. We use RS fMRI data to assess functional connectivity and for subject classification. We form ROIs in unique ways, with on average 5× fewer voxels per ROI than approaches using all anatomical region voxels for ROIs. Further, we aggregate voxel intensity values in unique ways for ROI-ROI correlation computation.

Our contributions are: (1) localized ROIs, one for each AAL-90 [4] region, defined by a single Hilbert curve [9] segment of a curve traversing a MNI-152 brain template [3] bounding box, (2) two novel *vector* representations of ROI voxel intensity magnitude values; a) *spatial*: the vectors consist of time-averaged ROI voxel intensity values, b) *spatial-temporal*: the vectors consist of concatenated ROI voxel time-series intensity values,(3) computationally efficient ROI-ROI correlation based CNN and Transformer models for accurate subject AD, MCI, and CN binary classification.

2   Related Work

The ML methods that have been applied to AD classification can broadly be grouped into approaches either using voxel intensity values directly, or ROI-ROI correlation matrices derived from voxel intensity values as input data. For the direct approach in [10] the brain slice voxel intensity values were converted to the PNG format and classification carried out on PNG encoded images. For 200 whole-brain time samples each having 48 slices 9600 image would be collected for each subject and 1,920,000 64 × 64 images for 200 subjects. In [11] it was reported that ResNet [12] applied to ImageNet [11] 1.2 M 224 × 224 images required 36 min using eight NVIDIA A100 GPUs having a combined peak FP32 performance of 156TF ($1TF = 10^{12}$ FP32 operations/second) and 1248TF using tensor cores [13]. This is 80–360 times slower than our reported training time in Table 2 using one NVIDIA K40 GPU with a peak performance of 4.29TF [14]. ML approaches based on ROI-ROI correlation matrices include SVMs, logistic regression, and random neural networks [15–20].

3   Dataset

We created three data sets from the ADNI (http://adni.loni.ucla.edu) and OASIS [21] Resting-State fMRI data sets for assessing ROI image intensity representation effectiveness for classification accuracy using small CNN and Transformer models for binary AD, MCI, and CN subject classification. One data set was created from each of the two data sets and a third larger data set by combining data from the two data sets to assess data set size impact on model performance. The ADNI data set of 140 whole brain samples each having 48 64 × 64 voxel slices for 302 subjects contain 101 AD subjects (33%), 97 MCI subjects (32%), and 104 CN subjects (34%). The OASIS dataset for of up to 164 whole-brain samples each having 36 64 × 64 voxel slices contains no MCI subjects, 149 (43%) AD subjects and 197 (57%) CN subjects (346 subjects in total). The combined data (Mixed) set of 648 subjects has 250 (39%) AD subjects, 97 (15%) MCI subjects, and 301 (46%) CN subjects.

4 Region of Interest (ROI)

After preprocessing including spatial smoothing and mapping [22, 23] each subjects brain to the MNI-152 template [3], we form spatially localized ROIs for the AAL90 brain atlas [4] based on segments of a Hilbert curve traversing a bounding box of the MNI-152 brain template. The choice of using a Hilbert curve for the 3D to 1D mapping of ROI Bold signal values was based on its locality preserving properties and its successful use for classification in [24]. We use a 64 × 64 × 64 bounding box for the MNI-152 brain template using 3.3 × 3.3 × 3.3 mm voxels. Adult brains typically contain about 31,000 (female) to 35,000 (male) voxels of this size corresponding to on average about 350–390 voxels per AAL90 region. For Hilbert curve segments representing an ROI, we report results for segment lengths of 101 and 201 voxels. Segment lengths of 51 voxels did not give satisfactory results and 301 voxel segments resulted in overlap for some ROIs. Segments were formed with equal length subsegments from a center-voxel located at the AAL90 regions center voxels.

We use three novel ways to derive ROI vector values from MNI-152 voxel intensity magnitude values: (1) spatial: the ROI vectors consist of time-averaged voxel intensity values for ROI Hilbert curve segment voxels, (2) spatial-temporal: the ROI vectors consist of concatenated time-series intensity values for all ROI Hilbert curve segment voxels. (3) temporal: ROI vectors consist of spatially averaged intensity values for the ROI Hilbert curve segment voxels. Other works have averaged voxel intensity values of all ROI voxels as defined by brain atlases, and hence differs from our temporal ROI vectors. Pearson correlation [25] is used for ROI-ROI vector correlations. With V(l,n) and V(l,m) denoting the intensity value of voxel l in ROI n and m respectively, $\rho(n, m)$ denoting the Pearson correlation of ROIs n and m and R the number of ROIs, the correlation for length L vectors is determined as:

$$\rho(n, m) = \frac{1}{(L-1)} \sum_{l=1}^{L} \frac{(V(l, n) - \mu(n))(V(l, m) - \mu(m))}{\sigma(n)\sigma(m)}, \text{ for } n, m \in [1, R] \quad (1)$$

$$\mu(r) = \frac{1}{L} \sum_{l=1}^{L} V(l, r) \text{ and } \sigma(r) = \text{sqrt}(\frac{1}{L} \sum_{l=1}^{L} (V(l, r) - \mu(n))^2 \text{ for } r \in [1, R] \quad (2)$$

with $\mu(r)$ being the mean intensity value of voxels in ROI r and $\sigma(r)$ being the standard deviation.

5   CNN Models

The input to the CNNs is the 90×90 ROI-ROI correlation matrices for each subject with one channel, the voxel intensity values. The number of output channels for the convolution layers in CNN-A is 4,8,16, respectively, each having 3×3 filters. The fourth layer is fully connected with 32 output channels. The last layer is fully connected with 2 output channels. The CNN-B has one convolution layer with 4 output channels and 2 fully connected layers with 8 and 2 output channels respectively. Thus, in CNN-A, and CNN-B the total number of parameters is 43,012 ($36 + 288 + 1,152 + 41,472 + 64$) and ($3 \times 3 \times 1 \times 4 + 44 \times 44 \times 4 \times 8 + 8 \times 2 = 62,004$) respectively. In IEEE FP32 data representation, the CNN-A model size is about 168 kiB and the CNN-B model about 242 kiB. Both CNN models are considerably smaller than many other CNN image classification models [12].

6   Transformer Model

To feed 2D data to the Transformer encoder [26, 27], each 2D data set is split into linearized patches. The resulting vector is passed to a linear layer to be embedded in a lower dimension. The Transformer linear layer includes matrix multiplication, in which patches sequences are multiplied with a learnable weight. With our focus on computational and memory efficiency, we chose patch sizes that result in square-like matrices. Specifically, we chose 10×10 patches for the correlation matrix, which results in 81×100 sequences. A sequence is fed into a linear layer and embedded to size 16. The sequence of size 81×16 is added to the position embedding vector which is a vector of constant numbers added to the sequence to keep the order of entities in the sequence. Our Transformer model has one encoder, with the most important components being a self-attention layer and a feed-forward layer [28]. The goal of self-attention is to capture the interaction among all 81 entities (tokens) by encoding each entity in terms of global contextual information. For a given entity in the sequence, the self-attention computes the dot-product of the query with all keys, which is then normalized using the SoftMax [29] operator to get the attention scores. To capsulate multiple complex relationships among different elements in the sequence, the multi-head attention is comprised of multi self-attention blocks. Each block has its own set of learnable weight matrices $\{W^{Q_i}, W^{K_i}, W^{V_i}\}$ where $i = 0, ..h$. In our model $h = 2$ and $d_q = d_k = dv = 8$. The outputs from two heads are concatenated into a single matrix and projected onto a weight matrix via a linear layer. The Transformer model has considerably fewer parameters than both our CNN models, as seen from Table 1. It requires about 26% more MACs than the CNN-B model but far fewer MACs than the CNN-A model (Fig. 1).

7   Experiments

To evaluate the classification accuracy of our CNN and Transformer models, five classification experiments were carried out: AD-CN-Mixed, AD-CN-OASIS, AD-CN-ADNI, MCI-CN-ADNI, MCI-AD-ADNI. In the triplet notation, the first two entries denote the binary classification carried out, and the last the data set used. In all experiments test

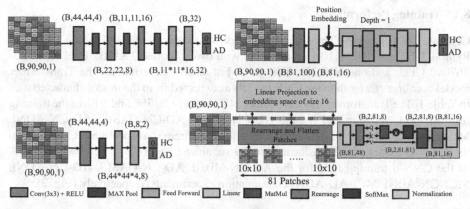

Fig. 1. Proposed CNN-A, CNN-B, and Transformer architecture

Table 1. Comparison of CNNs and Transformer architecture regarding memory footprint, and number of MACs

Model	#Params	#MAC	FP32 parameter memory
CNN-A	43,012	2,797,472	168 KB
CNN-B	62,004	707,136	242 KB
Transformer	9498	891,648	37.10 KB

set subjects were randomly chosen. Each experiment was repeated 30 times. In the AD-CN-Mixed experiment, the 97 MCI subjects were excluded resulting in a set with 551 subjects with test sets of 111 and training sets of 440 subjects. In the AD-CN-OASIS experiment, of the 346 OASIS subjects, test sets had 70 and training sets 276 subjects. In the AD-CN-ADNI experiment, of the 205 subjects classified as either AD or CN, test sets had 41 and training sets 164 subjects. In the MCI-CN-ADNI experiment, the data set size with AD subjects excluded was 201with test sets having 40 and training sets 161 subjects. In the MCI-AD-ADNI experiment, the ADNI subset of AD or MCI subjects is of size 198, with test sets having 39 and training sets 159 subjects.

8 Training

We use the Adam Optimizer [30] with a fixed learning rate of 0.001 for the CNN and Transformer models. Data augmentation was not used in any experiments. Models are trained for 15 epochs. In every epoch, batches of four matrices picked in order are used to ensure every matrix is used only once. In each epoch, we randomly permute matrix orders in the training set to assure matrix batches are different for every epoch.

8.1 Training Performance

CNN-A, CNN-B and the Transformer network were implemented in Pytorch 1.5.0 with Python 3.7.7 and CUDA 10.1 on a system with two 10 cores, 2.8 GHz Intel Xeon E5-2670v2 CPUs and one NVIDIA K40 GPU. For all five experiments, the Transformer model converges faster than the CNN models as expected from the model characteristics in Table 1. The Transformer model requires 14%, 14%, 11%, 7%, and 10% of the training time of the CNN-A model for the AD-CN-Mixed, AD-CN-OASIS, AD-CN-ADNI, MCI-CN-ADNI, MCI-AD-ADNI classification experiments, respectively. Compared to the CNN-B model, the Transformer model requires 13%, 14%, 9%, 10%, and 10% of the CNN-B training time for the AD-CN-Mixed, AD-CN-OASIS, AD-CN-ADNI, MCI-CN-ADNI, MCI-AD-ADNI classification experiments, respectively (Fig. 2).

Table 2. Mean and standard deviation of training times for the CNN-A, CNN-B, and Transformer models for our five classification experiments

Data set	Training time (s) + std (s)				
	CNN-B	CNN-A	Transformer	(Transformer/CNN-A)	(Transformer/CNN-B)
AD-CN-Mixed	201.72 ± 12.49	188.88 ± 21.47	**27.41 ± 8.40**	6.71X	7.35X
AD-CN-OASIS	121.00 ± 8.70	119.81 ± 9.30	**17.11 ± 7.70**	7.00X	7.07X
AD-CN-ANDI	65.10 ± 10.05	53.29 ± 22.26	**5.96 ± 0.78**	8.94X	10.92X
MCI-CN-ADNI	66.80 ± 5.06	93.48 ± 6.33	**6.75 ± 1.68**	13.84X	9.89X
MCI-AD-ADNI	63.70 ± 10.04	68.96 ± 3.67	**6.90 ± 1.65**	9.94X	9.23X

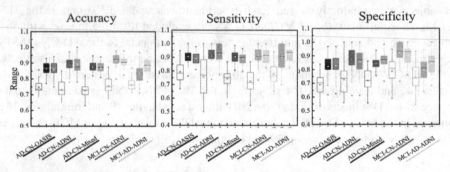

Fig. 2. Temporal correlation (T) (No fill), Spatial correlation (S) (Solid fill), Spatial-Temporal correlation (ST) (Pattern fill)

9 Classification Accuracy

We assessed the effectiveness of our BOLD signal ROI aggregation vectors on accuracy (ACC), sensitivity (SE), and specificity (SP) for each of our ML models for each of our five classification experiments.

Table 3. Best mean (%) and related standard deviation (%) of accuracy, sensitivity, and specificity for 30 randomly selected test sets for each of the AD-CN-Mixed, AD-CN-OASIS, AD-CN-ADNI, MCI-CN-ADNI and MCI-AD-ADNI classification experiments and our three voxel BOLD signal aggregations (S, ST, and T) for 101 and 201 ROI voxels

	CNN-A			CNN-B			Transformer		
	ACC(%)	SE(%)	SP(%)	ACC(%)	SE(%)	SP(%)	AC (%)	SE(%)	SP(%)
AD-CN-OASIS									
ST	84 ± 4 (101,201)	80 ± 9 (201)	88 ± 5 (101)	**86 ± 4 (101)**	**83 ± 8 (101)**	**90 ± 4 (101)**	86 ± 4 (101/201)	83 ± 8 (101/201)	89 ± 5 (101)
S	86 ± 5 (101)	82 ± 9 (101)	90 ± 7 (101)	87 ± 4 (101)	82 ± 9 (101)	90 ± 5 (101)	87 ± 4 (101)	85 ± 7 (101)	90 ± 5 (101)
T	69 ± 5 (101)	63 ± 11 (101)	76 ± 7 (201)	75 ± 5 (101)	69 ± 8 (101)	80 ± 7 (201)	77 ± 5 (101)	73 ± 10 (101)	79 ± 6 (201)
AD-CN-ADNI									
ST	87 ± 5 (101)	84 ± 8 (101)	90 ± 6 (101)	89 ± 5 (101)	87 ± 7 (201)	93 ± 6 (101)	87 ± 4 (101)	85 ± 8 (201)	89 ± 6 (101)
S	86 ± 5 (101)	82 ± 10 (101)	92 ± 6 (101)	89 ± 5 (101)	87 ± 9 (101)	91 ± 7 (101)	87 ± 4 (101)	87 ± 7 (101)	87 ± 7 (101)
T	64 ± 8 (101)	66 ± 12 (101)	65 ± 15 (201)	73 ± 7 (201)	73 ± 11 (201)	76 ± 14 (201)	74 ± 8 (101/201)	74 ± 18 (101)	74 ± 8 (201)
AD-CN-Mixed									
ST	86 ± 3 (101)	83 ± 6 (101)	89 ± 5 (101)	87 ± 3 (201)	87 ± 6 (201)	89 ± 4 (201)	87 ± 3 (201)	87 ± 6 (201)	89 ± 5 (101/201)
S	86 ± 3 (101)	83 ± 6 (101)	89 ± 4 (101)	88 ± 2 (101,201)	86 ± 5 (201)	90 ± 4 (101)	87 ± 3 (101/201)	85 ± 5 (101/201)	89 ± 5 (101/201)
T	69 ± 4 (101)	65 ± 8 (101)	72 ± 7 (201)	73 ± 4 (101,201)	72 ± 8 (201)	75 ± 5 (101)	73 ± 4 (101/201)	71 ± 7 (101)	75 ± 6 (201)
MCI-CN-ADNI									
ST	89 ± 4 (101)	90 ± 5 (201)	90 ± 5 (101)	90 ± 3 (201)	90 ± 7 (201)	91 ± 5 (201)	88 ± 5 (201)	88 ± 14 (201)	89 ± 11 (201)
S	92 ± 4 (101)	93 ± 6 (101)	91 ± 6 (101)	92 ± 4 (101)	92 ± 7 (101)	92 ± 6 (101)	90 ± 4 (201)	93 ± 6 (201)	88 ± 7 (201)
T	70 ± 6 (201)	73 ± 11 (201)	69 ± 9 (201)	75 ± 6 (201)	79 ± 9 (201)	72 ± 9 (201)	74 ± 5 (101)	77 ± 9 (101)	73 ± 13 (201)
MCI-AD-ADNI									
ST	86 ± 4 (101)	82 ± 9 (101)	90 ± 8 (101)	88 ± 4 (201)	84 ± 7 (201)	92 ± 5 (201)	76 ± 5 (201)	73 ± 11 (201)	79 ± 12 (201)
S	82 ± 5 (101)	81 ± 8 (201)	85 ± 10 (101)	84 ± 6 (101)	84 ± 8 (201)	90 ± 9 (101)	84 ± 5 (201)	80 ± 9 (201,101)	89 ± 8 (201)
T	76 ± 6 (101)	75 ± 10 (101)	78 ± 8 (101)	74 ± 8 (201)	77 ± 8 (201)	76 ± 11 (201)	73 ± 8 (101/201)	74 ± 11 (101)	72 ± 12 (201)

We also assessed the significance of the number of voxels (Hilbert curve segment lengths) used for ROIs. Table 3 summarizes the best mean and related standard deviation for 30 repetitions of each of the five experiments and our three signal aggregations for 101 and 201 ROI voxels. S, ST and T denote results for spatial, spatial-temporal and temporal BOLD signal aggregation. The outcome differences between the spatial and spatial-temporal ROI vector results are small. One or the other gives better results for the five classification experiments with no apparent pattern. The classification accuracy for ROI sizes 101 and 201 is comparable for all five classification experiments and the CNN and Transformer models. However, generally, the CNN-B model yields somewhat higher accuracy for 101 than for 201 size ROIs and CNN-A and Transformer models regardless of segment length. The results for sensitivity and specificity are somewhat more favorable for 101 than 201 size ROI and CNN-B than for CNN-A.

10 Conclusion

Convolution Neural Networks with 168 kiB parameter memory and a Transformer model with only 37 kiB parameter memory was shown to yield accuracies of 86–90%, sensitivity and specificity in the 82–93% and 88–93% range respectively for binary classification of AD/CN/MCI subjects. Training times were 188 (CNN) and 27 (Transformer) seconds on a NVIDIA K40 GPU for a dataset size of 551 subjects each represented by a ROI-ROI 90×90 correlation matrix. Thus, the Transformer model training time was about 15% of our least time-consuming CNN model and its memory requirement about 22% of memory the smallest CNN model for comparable outcomes.

We showed that about 100 voxels per ROI selected as Hilbert curve segments centered at AAL90 region center voxels were sufficient for our accuracy, sensitivity and specificity results with our spatial and spatial-temporal BOLD signal aggregations. Those two aggregations yielded similar results and better results than the typically used temporal aggregation of BOLD signals of all voxels in an anatomical ROI.

Acknowledgement. We are grateful for the University of Houston support that included resources provided by the UH-HPE Data Science Institute and thank members of the ACRL group for many helpful discussions. Access to the ADNI (funded by NIH Grant U01 AG024904 and DOD award W81XWH-12-2-0012) and OASIS (funded by NIH grants P50 AG00561, P30 NS09857781, P01 AG026276, P01 AG003991, R01 AG043434, UL1 TR000448, R01 EB009352) data is gratefully acknowledged.

References

1. Ogawa, S., Lee, T.M., Kay, A.R., Tank, D.W.: Brain magnetic resonance imaging with contrast dependent on blood oxygenation. Proc. Natl. Acad. Sci. **87**(24), 9868–9872 (1990)
2. Logothetis, N.K.: The neural basis of the blood–oxygen–level–dependent functional magnetic resonance imaging signal. Philos. Trans. R. Soc. London. Ser. B Biol. Sci. **357**(1424), 1003–1037 (2002)
3. Grabner, G., Janke, A.L., Budge, M.M., Smith, D., Pruessner, J., Collins, D.L.: Symmetric atlasing and model based segmentation: an application to the hippocampus in older adults. In: Larsen, R., Nielsen, M., Sporring, J. (eds.) MICCAI 2006. LNCS, vol. 4191, pp. 58–66. Springer, Heidelberg (2006). https://doi.org/10.1007/11866763_8
4. Tzourio-Mazoyer, N., et al.: Automated anatomical labeling of activations in SPM using a macroscopic anatomical parcellation of the MNI MRI single-subject brain. Neuroimage **15**(1), 273–289 (2002)

5. Fan, L., et al.: The human brainnetome atlas: a new brain atlas based on connectional architecture. Cereb. Cortex **26**(8), 3508–3526 (2016)
6. Craddock, R.C., James, G.A., Holtzheimer, P.E., III., Hu, X.P., Mayberg, H.S.: A whole brain fMRI atlas generated via spatially constrained spectral clustering. Hum. Brain Mapp. **33**(8), 1914–1928 (2012)
7. Biswal, B., Zerrin Yetkin, F., Haughton, V.M., Hyde, J.S.: Functional connectivity in the motor cortex of resting human brain using echo-planar MRI. Magn. Reson. Med. **34**(4), 537–541 (1995)
8. Beckmann, C.F., DeLuca, M., Devlin, J.T., Smith, S.M.: Investigations into resting-state connectivity using independent component analysis. Philos. Trans. R. Soc. B Biol. Sci. **360**(1457), 1001–1013 (2005)
9. Hilbert, D.: Über die stetige Abbildung einer Linie auf ein Flächenstück. In: Dritter Band: Analysis · Grundlagen der Mathematik · Physik Verschiedenes. Springer, Heidelberg (1935). https://doi.org/10.1007/978-3-662-38452-7_1
10. Odusami, M., Maskeliūnas, R., Damaševičius, R., Krilavičius, T.: Analysis of features of Alzheimer's disease: detection of early stage from functional brain changes in magnetic resonance images using a finetuned ResNet18 network. Diagnostics **11**(6), 1071 (2021)
11. https://mlcommons.org/en/training-normal-10/
12. He, K., Zhang, X., Ren, S., Sun, J.: Deep residual learning for image recognition. In: Proceedings of the IEEE Conference on Computer Vision and Pattern Recognition, pp. 770–778 (2016)
13. https://www.nvidia.com/content/dam/en-zz/Solutions/Data-Center/a100/pdf/nvidia-a100-datasheet.pdf
14. https://www.nvidia.com/content/dam/en-zz/Solutions/Data-Center/tesla-product-literature/TeslaK80-datasheet.pdf
15. Sarraf, S., DeSouza, D.D., Anderson, J., Tofighi, G.: DeepAD: Alzheimer's disease classification via deep convolutional neural networks using MRI and fMRI. BioRxiv 70441 (2016)
16. Kim, J., Calhoun, V.D., Shim, E., Lee, J.H.: Deep neural network with weight sparsity control and pre-training extracts hierarchical features and enhances classification performance: evidence from whole-brain resting-state functional connectivity patterns of schizophrenia. Neuroimage **124**, 127–146 (2016)
17. Shi, Y., Zeng, W., Deng, J., Nie, W., Zhang, Y.: The identification of Alzheimer's disease using functional connectivity between activity voxels in resting-state fMRI data. IEEE J. Transl. Eng. Heal. Med. **8**, 1–11 (2020)
18. Challis, E., Hurley, P., Serra, L., Bozzali, M., Oliver, S., Cercignani, M.: Gaussian process classification of Alzheimer's disease and mild cognitive impairment from resting-state fMRI. Neuroimage **112**, 232–243 (2015)
19. Chen, G., et al.: Classification of Alzheimer disease, mild cognitive impairment, and normal cognitive status with large-scale network analysis based on resting-state functional MR imaging. Radiology **259**(1), 213–221 (2011)
20. Bi, X.A., Jiang, Q., Sun, Q., Shu, Q., Liu, Y.: Analysis of Alzheimer's disease based on the random neural network cluster in fMRI. Front. Neuroinform. **12**, 60 (2018)
21. LaMontagne, P.J., et al.: OASIS-3: longitudinal neuroimaging, clinical, and cognitive dataset for normal aging and Alzheimer disease. MedRxiv (2019)
22. Studholme, C., Hill, D.L., Hawkes, D.J.: An overlap invariant entropy measure of 3D medical image alignment. Pattern Recognit. **32**(1), 71–86 (1999)
23. Ashburner, J., Friston, K.J.: Unified segmentation. Neuroimage **26**(3), 839–851 (2005)
24. Sakoglu, U., Bhupati, L., Beheshti, N., Tsekos, N., Johnsson, L.: An adaptive space-filling curve trajectory for ordering 3D datasets to 1D: application to brain magnetic resonance

imaging data for classification. In: Krzhizhanovskaya, V.V., et al. (eds.) ICCS 2020. LNCS, vol. 12139, pp. 635–646. Springer, Cham (2020). https://doi.org/10.1007/978-3-030-50420-5_48

25. Benesty, J., Chen, J., Huang, Y., Cohen, I.: Pearson correlation coefficient. In: Noise Reduction in Speech Processing, pp. 1–4. Springer, Heidelberg (2009). https://doi.org/10.1007/978-3-642-00296-0_5

26. Khan, S., Naseer, M., Hayat, M., Zamir, S.W., Khan, F.S., Shah, M.: Transformers in vision: a survey. arXiv Prepr. arXiv2101.01169 (2021)

27. Dosovitskiy, A., et al.: An image is worth 16x16 words: transformers for image recognition at scale. arXiv Prepr. arXiv2010.11929 (2020)

28. Vaswani, A., et al.: Attention is all you need (2017)

29. Jang, E., Gu, S., Poole, B.: Categorical reparameterization with gumbel-softmax. arXiv Prepr. arXiv1611.01144 (2016)

30. Kingma, D.P., Ba, J.: Adam: a method for stochastic optimization. arXiv Prepr. arXiv1412.6980 (2014)

An Efficient Defending Mechanism Against Image Attacking on Medical Image Segmentation Models

Linh D. Le[✉] [iD], Huazhu Fu[iD], Xinxing Xu[iD], Yong Liu[iD], Yanyu Xu,
Jiawei Du[iD], Joey T. Zhou[iD], and Rick Goh[iD]

Institute of High Performance Computing, A*STAR, Singapore, Singapore
linhld@ihpc.a-star.edu.sg

Abstract. Image attacking has been studied for a long time. However, in reality, the number of research on defending against the attacks on segmentation models is still limited especially for medical imaging. To fill this research gap, we propose a novel defending mechanism against adversarial attacks for the segmentation models. We focus on segmentation as robustness improvement on segmentation is much more challenging due to its dense nature, and segmentation is at the center of medical imaging tasks. In this paper, we are the first time to employ Transformer as a technique to protect the segmentation models from attacks. Our result on several medical well-known benchmark datasets shows that the proposed defending mechanism to enhance the segmentation models is effective with high scores and better compared to other strong methods.

Keywords: Defending · Adversarial attacking · Medical image segmentation · Transformer

1 Introduction

We provide a use case that attacked medical images that are vulnerable to the segmentation model. This will lead doctors to misdiagnose the diseases when relying on those models. e.g. doctors may conclude the infectious lung images to be non-infectious when doing a Covid patient's examination based on the segmented result. Therefore in this work, we present a study about a defending mechanism for those segmentation tasks.

Some defending against attack methods can be listed out. [11] proposes to denoise the adversarial images by subtracting the adversarial to the reconstructed residual image and the method called high level guided denoiser (HGD) has worked well for the NIPS 2017 challenge. [22](Feat) applies non-local means and filters along with adversarial training for denoising the adversarial images. In general, adversarial training is a popular technique that was proved to be efficient in terms of error rate. However, the training still takes time and this method is more suitable for applying to adversarial attacks where the images are

X. Xu et al. (Eds.): REMIA 2022, LNCS 13543, pp. 65–74, 2022.
https://doi.org/10.1007/978-3-031-16876-5_7

generated during training so that the main defender model can learn the gradient from the generating process. In our work, we propose the training mechanism where the attacked images are generated before training the defender model. We also take the performance of the target model on the original clean image into account.

For segmentation tasks where the output is different from classification because of the per-pixel classification target hence adversarial examples are harder to generate. To attack segmentation models, currently, there are many methods. [15] uses CGAN to modify semantic features of images but when applied to medical datasets the quality is unacceptable due to the limitation of the current GAN model. [12] introduce a frequency-based defending for Adaptive Segmentation Mask Attack [14]. On the other hand, this kind of attack results in unchanged the main part of the adversarial image but results in the four margins of it perturbed and the image size is changed. Therefore, it cannot be considered to be good in terms of perceptual quality. Crafting adversarial on medical color image datasets like REFUGEE fundus and brain CT scan dataset is much harder. Normal methods like DAG [23], IFGSM [10], CW [3], PGD [13] often fail in the context of spoiling segmentation models. Scaling attack [21] has been known as an efficient technique to sabotage the scaling image process and thereafter, was discovered to enhance the perceptual quality of adversarial attack [6]. Following that, we also discover the good acquired perceptual quality through a minor modification of the scaling attack. To achieve the best attack result we use DAG, and IFGSM to only generate gray medical images on the Covid dataset.

2   Our Methods

2.1   Improve Robustness Against Adversarial Example for Segmentation Models

Proposed Defending Mechanism. We introduce the transformer-based defender model to preprocess the input images which are attacked-unknown before feeding them to target segmentation models. Figure 1 shows our new mechanism (DefTrans) to protect the segmentation models against attacked images. Corresponding clean images are also learned in conjunction with the attacked samples to assure the preservative performance on not only attacked images but normal images. During training the defender, the target model will be fixed parameters. Here we use UNet(UN) [16] as the model to calculate the output of the softmax function as UN has been known for common segmentation tasks. Input images for training include generated attacked images and the corresponding clean images. We propose two types of loss functions for the usage of the optimizing the defender are Triple Resemble loss:

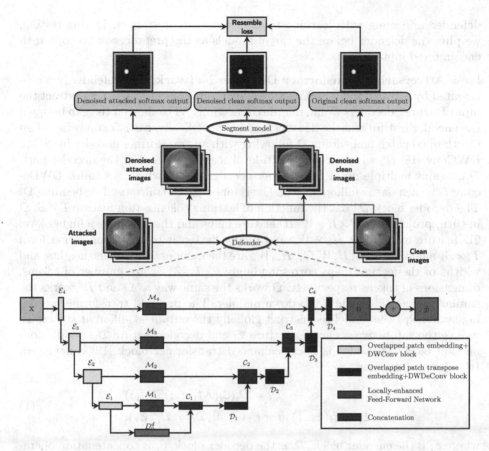

Fig. 1. New defending mechanism for segmentation models. In our experiment, Segmodel is a pretrained UNet. Attacked and clean images after passing through defender $\mathcal{D}$ will be given out corresponding denoised images to pass to Segmodel. The probability output after the softmax layer of Segmodel on denoised images and clean images will be used to calculate loss during the training phase.

$$\mathcal{TR} = ||f_s(x) - f_s(\hat{x}_{adv})||^2 + ||f_s(x) - f_s(\hat{x}_{cl})||^2$$

and Foursome Resemble loss:

$$\mathcal{FR} = ||f_s(x) - f_s(\hat{x}_{adv})||^2 + ||f_s(x) - f_s(\hat{x}_{cl})||^2 - ||f_s(x) - f_s(x_{adv})||^2,$$

where f_s is the output softmax of the pretrained UN given input images, x is input clean image, $\hat{x}_{adv}$ is output denoised image from defender $\mathcal{D}$ after denoise input adversarial image x_{adv}, $\hat{x}_{cl}$ is output denoised image from clean image x. $\mathcal{TR}$ loss is to force the defender to learn to denoise correctly so that the output segmentation result of the denoised adversarial images looks like the clean image segmentation output and maintains the same similarity with the output of denoised clean images. $\mathcal{FR}$ is another modification for sharpening the defender in dealing with learning tougher noise circumstances. During testing, we plug the defender before the target models as the preprocessor to cope with encountered input images.

New Adversarial Transformer Defender Network. The defender $\mathbb{D}$ is represented by a Transformer architecture which comprises encoders $\mathcal{E}$ to extract the input features, decoders $\mathcal{D}$ and middle connections $\mathcal{M}$ to shorten the gap between the encoder feature and the decoder feature. Specifically, each $\mathcal{E}_i$ comprises of an Overlapped patch embedding $\mathfrak{O}$ following with an transformer encoder block are DWConv [18] D^e which encode multi-level scale features. For the decoder part, $\mathcal{D}$ contains multiple novel transformer decoder blocks which are called DWDeconv D^d, each one is followed by an Overlapped patch transposed embedding $\hat{\mathfrak{O}}$. The decoder block D^d has the function of learning tokenization feature $\hat{T} \times \hat{Z}$. $\hat{\mathfrak{O}}$ in turn, project it to $C \times H \times W$ 2D feature maps and then produce a higher level 2D feature maps $C_* \times H_* \times W_*$ and finally flatten it to the tokenization form $\hat{T}_* \times \hat{Z}_*$ again. Here, C, H, W, C_*, H_*, W_* are the number of channels, heights, and widths of the feature maps correspondingly. $\hat{T}, \hat{T}_*, \hat{Z}, \hat{Z}_*$ are number of tokens, dimensions of tokens respectively. $\mathfrak{O}$ works the same way as $\hat{\mathfrak{O}}$ and D^e works the similar way as D^d but in a top-down manner. The pyramid transformer decoding style helps the model reconstruct globally the output at different stages. To reduce the gap between encoder feature $\mathfrak{E}_i$ and decoder feature $\mathfrak{D}_i$, middle connection block $\mathcal{M}_i$ which is Local enhanced transformer block [19] is deployed. In a detailed manner,

$$\mathfrak{D}_i = \mathcal{D}_i(\mathcal{C}_i(\mathcal{M}_i(\mathfrak{E}_i), \mathfrak{D}_{i-1}))$$
$$\mathfrak{E}_i = \mathcal{E}_i(\mathfrak{E}_{i-1}), for\, i = [1,4]; \mathfrak{D}_0 = D_0^d(\mathfrak{E}_1), \qquad (1)$$

where $\mathcal{E}_i$ is the encoder block, $\mathcal{D}_i$ is the decoder block, $\mathcal{C}_i$ is concatenation operator, $\mathcal{M}_i$ is the middle connection block at level i and D_0^d is the bottleneck block. The denoised image $\hat{x}$ is formulated by $\hat{x} = n + x$, where $n = \mathfrak{D}_4$ is the learnt noise image.

2.2   Attacking Segmentation Model

Attacking Algorithms. In our work, Segnet (SN) [1], UNet, DenseNet (DN) [8] DeepLabV3+ with Resnet101, Mobilenet backbone [4] and AgNet (AN) [26] are used as target models. Depending on the result of which models give the best segmentation output, some of them are selected to do experiments on specific datasets. To train the target models and generate the adversarial images from the corresponding models, including SN, UN, DN, DeepLabV3+ combine loss $\mathcal{C}$ which is the simplification of [17] has been used, except for AgNet which takes in Dice loss as the segmentation loss function.

Non-gradient Based Attack. We have scaling attacks modified to use for a different objective. Scaling attack [6] takes the input source image $\mathcal{S}$ and the target image $\mathcal{T}$ then produce the wrong downscaling version of $\mathcal{S}$, $\mathfrak{S}$ that $\mathfrak{S}$ looks similar to $\mathcal{S}$. Compared to the original attack design in which the final output of the attacking process is the target image after the downscaling process by some other popular resizing library is spoiled, we have applied PIL resizing algorithm in replacing that. By doing so, from mixup image $\mathfrak{M}$, it gives out the final output image $\mathfrak{T}$ that $\mathfrak{T}$ resembles the target image $\mathcal{T}$ while still preserving the information from $\mathcal{S}$ (Fig. 1).

Model Gradients Based Attack. To make sure that generated adversarial examples look like the real data, we have used scaling attacks for all datasets, DAG, and IFGSM only for the gray dataset. We found through experiments that IFGSM synthesizes images much closer to the clean version than DAG and in general both DAG and IFGSM can be considered to be weaker attacks compare to scaling attacks. For the DAG generating, we use two kinds of target pixels selection. Type I is to target all pixels in the attacked image to be the background. Type II is to swap between all of class 1 pixels to class 0(background) and vice versa. For IFGSM, only Type I is used for the best-generated image quality. Figure 3 shows how targeting pixels are defined to be targeted on the attacks.

3 Experiment and Results

In the experiments, Covid lung is used as the gray dataset from [9]. This dataset contains 20 labeled COVID-19 CT scans. Left lung, right lung, and infections are labeled by two radiologists and verified by an experienced radiologist. We train the segmentation model with the infectious labels. The dataset is split patient-based with the number of samples training/validating/testing being 1816/631/1073. We also use the fundus dataset [5] and brain MRI [2] as color datasets. The fundus dataset consists of images of glaucoma disease and the tasks are glaucoma detection and optic disc/cup segmentation from the REFUGEE challenge. This data includes 400 images for training, validating, and testing respectively. For the brain dataset from the Kaggle competition, the number of samples training/validating/testing is 2501/625/803 split from the original set. The training, validating, and testing dataset for the denoiser is generated from the same original clean images for those procedures on target models. All input images are resized to 256*256 pixels before doing the following experiments. The targeted segmentation models and defenders are all trained on 100 epochs. Adam optimizer is employed with the default parameters to train both target models and defenders. The models are trained under the NVIDIA GeForce RTX 3090 hardware using Pytorch framework. All models are selected based on the best evaluation epoch.

To train the defender for the scaling attack, generated images from the training and validation set are employed with the corresponding clean images. For generating scaling attack examples, we use a single brain CT image as the source image and the images from the experiment datasets play the target role. Normally the medical images often contain meta text information like measurement

Table 1. The defending result on scaling attack for fundus dataset. Metrics: Dice score.

Tg models	SegNet				UNet				DenseNet			
	Before df	HGD	Feat	Ours	Before df	HGD	Feat	Ours	Before df	HGD	Feat	Ours
Origin	0.74	0.35	0.43	**0.73**	0.80	0.25	0.33	**0.80**	0.74	0.28	0.33	**0.76**
Attack	0.22	0.33	0.43	**0.73**	0.22	0.33	0.33	**0.80**	0.23	0.31	0.33	**0.76**

Tg models	AgNet				DeepLabV3+_Resn101				Avg		
	Before df	HGD	Feat	Ours	Before df	HGD	Feat	Ours	HGD	Feat	Ours
Origin	0.92	0.48	0.61	**0.92**	0.81	0.28	0.38	**0.81**	0.33	0.42	**0.80**
Attack	0.30	0.34	0.60	**0.92**	0.25	0.33	0.37	**0.81**	0.33	0.41	**0.80**

device name, specifications, examination date, imaging modalities, and patient info. Inspired by that, the chosen brain CT contains some kinds of those text and therefore the attacked images also displayed those text in a background manner, and are hard to distinguish whether they are attacked. We perform scaling attacks and defend on the fundus, brain MRI and Covid lung dataset. To train the defender for DAG and IFGSM, we generate adversarial images among all kinds of target models and mask target types and randomly select one among them as input adversarial images to formulate the adversarial, clean pairs during training. In the setting to generate adversarial images, the number of iterations is 30, γ is 0.5 for DAG and ϵ is 0.03 for IFGSM.

3.1   Evaluation

Robustness on Attack Images. The results of scaling attack on fundus(Table 1), brain(Table 2) and lung(Table 3) dataset show that the attack has successfully degraded the target models with a high success rate. The dice score of target models on scaling attack images is in common much lower than on the original clean images. For adversarial images generated by DAG and IFGSM on the lung dataset, the attack results are in lower performance, this shows that scaling attack is more threatening than DAG and IFGSM. Compare with the result after using the defense mechanism, Table 1 shows that the defender has improved the robustness of target models obviously in general. Our defending results for scaling attack on all datasets display the good reconstruction image from scaling attack and sometimes the dice score after defending are even higher than the original on clean images. Besides, our results are by far better than Feat [22] and HGD [11] for all datasets in common. Only on the brain dataset, with DeepLabV3+_MobileNet target model, our results are lower than Feat. Our DefTrans model also takes less time for training, compared to the adversarial training with feature denoising by Feat [22]. The success of the framework is credited mainly to the Pyramid transformer encoding-decoding architecture of the defender. Besides, with the Resemble loss, which includes the output of the denoised clean images from the segmentation model, the framework can preserve the segmentation result on original clean images.

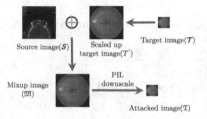

Fig. 2. Scaling attack.

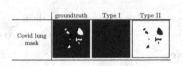

Fig. 3. Selected target pixels corresponding to classes. Type I indicates all pixels are assigned a false class as background. Type II indicates swapping all pixels belonging to class 0 to class 1 and vice versa.

Table 2. Scaling attack and defending on segmentation models result for brain dataset. Metrics: Dice score.

Target models		Origin	Attack	Target models		Origin	Attack
SegNet	Before df	0.87	0.41	DeepLabV3+ _MobileNet	Before df	0.91	0.39
	HGD	0.67	0.68		HGD	0.62	0.61
	Feat	0.70	0.70		Feat	**0.81**	**0.81**
	Ours	**0.82**	**0.81**		Ours	0.76	0.75
UNet	Before df	0.85	0.41	DenseNet	Before df	0.81	0.46
	HGD	0.71	0.71		HGD	0.71	0.71
	Feat	0.75	0.75		Feat	0.70	0.69
	Ours	**0.79**	**0.79**		Ours	**0.86**	**0.87**
Avg	HGD	0.68	0.68				
	Feat	0.74	0.74				
	Ours	**0.81**	**0.81**				

The defending results of our DefTrans on DAG and IFGSM (Table 3) also surpass Feat and HGD although they are lower compared to scaling attacks. This is because the scaling attack has not changed much the morphological of the lung gray images and therefore should be easier to defend against especially for our DefTrans. Compare to the other works [7,24], our mechanism is capable of protecting multiple target models by training just one time rather than being only a rigid segmentation model. Figure 4 displays some examples of our results.

Table 3. Defending result on different segmentation models using scaling attack, DAG and IFGSM for Covid lung dataset. Metrics: Dice score.

Target models	Attacks	scaling		DAG			IFGSM	
		Origin	Attack	Origin	Type I	Type II	Origin	Type I
AgNet	Before df	0.85	0.25	0.85	0.55	0.69	0.85	0.60
	HGD	0.54	0.51	0.54	0.54	0.55	0.57	0.56
	Feat	0.64	0.63	0.55	0.55	0.55	0.55	0.55
	Ours	**0.84**	**0.83**	**0.80**	**0.69**	**0.80**	**0.84**	**0.57**
UNet	Before df	0.82	0.25	0.82	0.54	0.51	0.57	0.57
	HGD	0.57	0.57	0.57	0.57	0.57	0.50	0.50
	Feat	0.56	0.56	0.57	0.57	0.57	0.51	0.51
	Ours	**0.81**	**0.79**	**0.78**	**0.67**	**0.60**	**0.82**	**0.57**
DenseNet	Before df	0.80	0.25	0.80	0.53	0.43	0.80	0.57
	HGD	0.57	0.57	0.57	0.57	0.57	0.51	0.51
	Feat	0.62	0.63	0.56	0.56	0.56	0.56	0.56
	Ours	**0.79**	**0.76**	**0.73**	**0.66**	**0.60**	**0.79**	**0.60**
DeepLabV3+ _Resnet101	Before df	0.77	0.26	0.77	0.63	0.75	0.77	0.56
	HGD	0.57	0.57	0.57	0.57	0.57	0.54	0.54
	Feat	0.57	0.57	0.66	0.63	0.65	0.63	0.62
	Ours	**0.72**	**0.71**	**0.74**	**0.72**	**0.73**	**0.75**	**0.74**
Avg	HGD	0.56	0.56	0.56	0.56	0.57	0.53	0.53
	Feat	0.60	0.60	0.59	0.58	0.58	0.56	0.56
	Ours	**0.79**	**0.77**	**0.76**	**0.69**	**0.68**	**0.80**	**0.62**

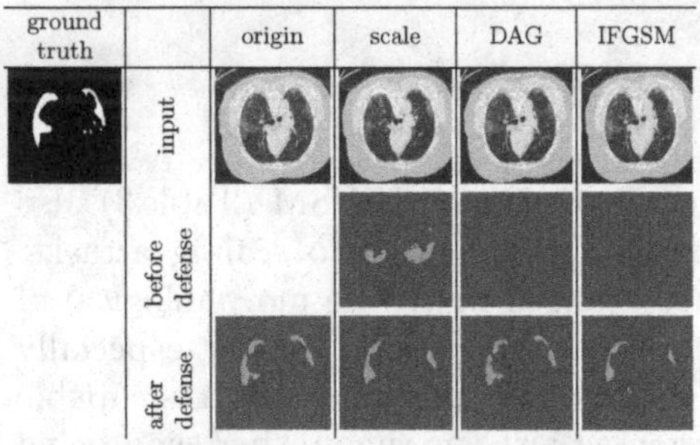

Fig. 4. Demonstration of denoising effect on different types of attacked methods compared on the Covid lung dataset. Target model: DeepLabV3+

Table 4. Perceptual quality.

Attack	Dataset	SSIM	FSIM
Scaling	Fundus	0.93	0.96
	Brain	0.98	0.98
	Lung	0.95	0.96
DAG	Lung	0.95	0.98
IFGSM	Lung	0.92	0.99

The Perceptual Quality of Attacked Images. For the perceptual quality of generated adversarial examples, the well-known metrics, structural similarity index (SSIM) [20] and feature similarity index(FSIM) [25] are used to compare the similarity of the generated image with the original test image. From Table 4, we can acknowledge that the perceptual quality of generated attacked images on all datasets is good with the SSIM and FSIM index always above 0.90. The perceptual quality of the scaling attack also depends on the source image that is used to attack and the best choice in our experiment is a dark background image. In practice, any kind of source image that fit the purpose and the target datasets can be employed.

4   Conclusions

In this paper, for the first time defending against image attacking in terms of both model gradients based and non-gradient based is studied for image segmentation. Moreover, a new defending mechanism to improve those models' robustness on attacks has been presented. This work is expected to contribute to the medical AI model's security and other application aspects.

Acknowledgements. This work was supported by A*STAR Advanced Manufacturing and Engineering (AME) Programmatic Fund (A20H4b0141);

References

1. Badrinarayanan, V., Kendall, A., Cipolla, R.: SegNet: a deep convolutional encoder-decoder architecture for image segmentation. CVPR, pp. 1–13 (2015)
2. Buda, M., AshirbaniSaha, Mazurowski, M.A.: Association of genomic subtypes of lower-grade gliomas with shape features automatically extracted by a deep learning algorithm. https://www.kaggle.com/mateuszbuda/lgg-mri-segmentation
3. Carlini, N., Wagner, D.: Towards evaluating the robustness of neural networks. In: IEEE Symposium on Security and Privacy (SP), pp. 1–15 (2017)
4. Chen, L.C., Zhu, Y., Papandreou, G., Schroff, F., Adam, H.: Encoder-decoder with atrous separable convolution for semantic image segmentation. In: ECCV, pp. 1–14 (2018)
5. FeiLi, et al.: Refuge: retinal fundus glaucoma challenge. https://refuge.grand-challenge.org/REFUGE2Download/
6. Gao, Y., Fawaz, K.: Scale-Adv: a joint attack on image-scaling and machine learning classifiers. CC, pp. 1–32 (2021)
7. He, X., Yang, S., Li, G., Li, H., Chang, H., Yu, Y.: Non-local context encoder: robust biomedical image segmentation against adversarial attacks. In: AAAI, pp. 3–5 (2019)
8. Huang, G., Liu, Z., van der Maaten, L., Weinberger, K.Q.: Densely connected convolutional networks. In: CVPR, pp. 1–9 (2017)
9. Jun, M., et al.: COVID-19 CT lung and infection segmentation dataset. https://zenodo.org/record/3757476#.YhoKnOhBzDd
10. Kurakin, A., Goodfellow, I.J., Bengio, S.: Adversarial machine learning at scale. ICLR, pp. 3–4 (2017)

11. Liao, F., Liang, M., Dong, Y., Pang, T., Huy, X., Zhu, J.: Defense against adversarial attacks using high-level representation guided denoiser. In: CVPR, pp. 1–8 (2018)
12. Liu, Q., et al.: Defending deep learning-based biomedical image segmentation from adversarial attacks: a low-cost frequency refinement approach. In: Martel, A.L., et al. (eds.) MICCAI 2020. LNCS, vol. 12264, pp. 342–351. Springer, Cham (2020). https://doi.org/10.1007/978-3-030-59719-1_34
13. Madry, A., Makelov, A., Schmidt, L., Tsipras, D., Vladu, A.: Towards deep learning models resistant to adversarial attacks. In: ICLR, pp. 3–4 (2019)
14. Ozbulak, U., Van Messem, A., De Neve, W.: Impact of adversarial examples on deep learning models for biomedical image segmentation. In: Shen, S., et al. (eds.) MICCAI 2019. LNCS, vol. 11765, pp. 300–308. Springer, Cham (2019). https://doi.org/10.1007/978-3-030-32245-8_34
15. Qiu, H., Xiao, C., Yang, L., Yan, X., Lee, H., Li, B.: SemanticAdv: generating adversarial examples via attribute-conditioned image editing. In: Vedaldi, A., Bischof, H., Brox, T., Frahm, J.-M. (eds.) ECCV 2020. LNCS, vol. 12359, pp. 19–37. Springer, Cham (2020). https://doi.org/10.1007/978-3-030-58568-6_2
16. Ronneberger, O., Fischer, P., Brox, T.: U-Net: convolutional networks for biomedical image segmentation. In: Navab, N., Hornegger, J., Wells, W.M., Frangi, A.F. (eds.) MICCAI 2015. LNCS, vol. 9351, pp. 234–241. Springer, Cham (2015). https://doi.org/10.1007/978-3-319-24574-4_28
17. Roy, A.G., Conjeti, S., Sheet, D., Katouzian, A., Navab, N., Wachinger, C.: Error corrective boosting for learning fully convolutional networks with limited data. In: Descoteaux, M., Maier-Hein, L., Franz, A., Jannin, P., Collins, D.L., Duchesne, S. (eds.) MICCAI 2017. LNCS, vol. 10435, pp. 231–239. Springer, Cham (2017). https://doi.org/10.1007/978-3-319-66179-7_27
18. Wang, W., et al.: PVT v2: Improved baselines with Pyramid Vision Transformer. Comput. Vis. Media 8, 1–10 (2022). https://doi.org/10.1007/s41095-022-0274-8
19. Wang, Z., Cun, X., Bao, J., Zhou, W., Liu, J., Li, H.: Uformer: a general u-shaped transformer for image restoration. arXiv:abs/2106.03106, pp. 1–8 (2021)
20. Wang, Z., Simoncelli, E.P., Bovik, A.C.: Multi-scale structural similarity for image quality assessment. In: ACSSC, pp. 1–4 (2003)
21. Xiao, Q., Chen, Y., Shen, C., Chen, Y., Li, K.: Seeing is not believing: camouflage attacks on image scaling algorithms. In: 28th USENIX Security Symposium, USENIX Security 2019, Santa Clara, CA, USA, pp. 1–32 (2019)
22. Xie, C., Wu, Y., van der Maaten, L., Yuille, A., He, K.: Feature denoising for improving adversarial robustness. In: CVPR, pp. 2–8 (2019)
23. Xie, C., Wang, J., Zhang, Z., Zhou, Y., Xie1, L., Yuille, A.: Adversarial examples for semantic segmentation and object detection. In: ICCV, pp. 1–12 (2017)
24. Xu, X., Zhao, H., Jia, J.: Dynamic divide-and-conquer adversarial training for robust semantic segmentation. In: CVPR, pp. 2–8 (2020)
25. Zhang, L., Zhang, L., Mou, X., Zhang, D.: FSIM: a feature similarity index for image quality assessment. IEEE Trans. Image Process. pp. 1–19 (2011)
26. Zhang, S., et al.: Attention guided network for retinal image segmentation. In: Shen, D., et al. (eds.) MICCAI 2019. LNCS, vol. 11764, pp. 797–805. Springer, Cham (2019). https://doi.org/10.1007/978-3-030-32239-7_88

Leverage Supervised and Self-supervised Pretrain Models for Pathological Survival Analysis via a Simple and Low-cost Joint Representation Tuning

Quan Liu[1,2], Can Cui[1,2], Ruining Deng[1,2], Zuhayr Asad[1,2], Tianyuan Yao[1,2], Zheyu Zhu[1,2], and Yuankai Huo[1,2(✉)]

[1] Vanderbilt University, Nashville, TN 37215, USA
[2] Vanderbilt University Medical Center, Nashville, TN 37215, USA
yuankai.huo@vanderbilt.edu

Abstract. The large-scale pretrained models from terabyte-level (TB) data are now broadly used in feature extraction, model initialization, and transfer learning in pathological image analyses. Most existing studies have focused on developing more powerful pretrained models, which are increasingly unscalable for academic institutes. Very few, if any, studies have investigated how to take advantage of existing, yet heterogeneous, pretrained models for downstream tasks. As an example, our experiments elucidated that self-supervised models (e.g., contrastive learning on the entire The Cancer Genome Atlas (TCGA) dataset) achieved a superior performance compared with supervised models (e.g., ImageNet pretraining) on a classification cohort. Surprisingly, it yielded an inferior performance when it was translated to a cancer prognosis task. Such a phenomenon inspired us to explore how to leverage the already trained supervised and self-supervised models for pathological survival analysis. In this paper, we present a simple and low-cost joint representation tuning (JRT) to aggregate task-agnostic vision representation (supervised ImageNet pretrained models) and pathological specific feature representation (self-supervised TCGA pretrained models) for downstream tasks. Our contribution is in three-fold: (1) we adapt and aggregate classification-based supervised and self-supervised representation to survival prediction via joint representation tuning, (2) comprehensive analyses on prevalent strategies of pretrained models are conducted, (3) the joint representation tuning provides a simple, yet computationally efficient, perspective to leverage large-scale pretrained models for both cancer diagnosis and prognosis. The proposed JRT method improved the c-index from 0.705 to 0.731 on the TCGA brain cancer survival dataset. The feature-direct JRT (f-JRT) method achieved 60× training speedup while maintaining 0.707 c-index score.

Keywords: Self-supervised learning · Representation tuning · Prognosis analysis · Pathology

© The Author(s), under exclusive license to Springer Nature Switzerland AG 2022
X. Xu et al. (Eds.): REMIA 2022, LNCS 13543, pp. 75–84, 2022.
https://doi.org/10.1007/978-3-031-16876-5_8

1   Introduction

Supervised pretrained models (e.g., on ImageNet [14] and BiT [17]) have been regarded as a powerful feature extractor and weight initializer in pathological image analysis [5,12]. However, it is resource-intensive to collect the large-scale annotated images, especially for gigapixel Whole Slide Images (WSIs) [7,9]. Without requiring annotations, self-supervised learning (SSL) approaches are leading to a paradigm shift in large-scale pretraining for histopathological image analysis from visual inspection to more accurate quantitative assessment [6,16,28,29], with the rapid growth of publicly available large-scale datasets (e.g., The Cancer Genome Atlas (TCGA) [26], and Pathology AI Platform (PAIP) [13]). In a recent study, Wang et al. [28] utilized the entire TCGA and PAIP dataset to perform a self-supervised pretraining via a vision transformer, called TransPath. TransPath learned the pathological domain-specific information and achieved superior tissue classification performance.

However, most existing studies focused on developing more powerful pretrained models [2,4,19,24], whose resource consumption is increasingly unscalable for academic institutes. Very few, if any, studies have investigated how to take advantage of existing, yet heterogeneous pretrained models for better performance on downstream tasks. As an example, the pathological data-optimized

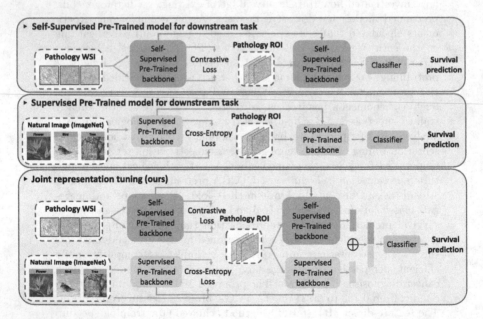

Fig. 1. Model pipeline. In the top section, self-supervised model is pretrained with pathology WSIs and finetuned on pathology images for survival prediction. Middle section is supervised pretrained model with natural images of ImageNet and finetuned on pathology images. Our JRT method aggregates both pretrained models to achieve better downstream task performance.

contrastive learning model TransPath [28] achieved a superior performance compared with supervised models (e.g., ImageNet pretrained) on a classification cohort (Table 2). **Surprisingly, it yielded a inferior performance when it was translated to a cancer prognosis task.** Such phenomenon inspired us to explore how to leverage the already trained supervised and self-supervised models for pathological survival analysis [15, 23, 31].

In this paper, we propose a simple joint representation tuning (JRT) approach to aggregate task-agnostic vision representation (supervised ImageNet pretrained models) and pathological specific representation (self-supervised TCGA pretrained models) for downstream tasks (Fig. 1). This study also evaluated the different strategies as well as their performance of using heterogeneous pretrained models. The feature-direct JRT (f-JRT) that directly finetune the joint feature representations without 1) encoder network, 2) data augmentation, and 3) large memory consumption, achieved 60× speedup with decent performance on the survival analysis.

The contribution of this paper is in three-fold:

- The JRT method adapts and aggregates the task-agnostic vision representation (supervised ImageNet pretrained models) and pathological specific features presentation (self-supervised pretrained models) for better performance on downstream tasks.
- Comprehensive analyses on prevalent strategies of using heterogeneous pretrained models are conducted as a reference for the community.
- The joint representation tuning provides a simple, yet computationally efficient perspective to leverage large-scale pretained models for both cancer diagnosis and prognosis without extra resource-intensive pretraining.

2 Methods

The overall framework of the proposed JRT approach is presented in Fig. 1. We have also conducted a comprehensive analyses to evaluate a variety of (1) pretraining approaches, (2) feature extraction and finetuning strategies, (3) joint representation tuning methods, and (4) downstream tasks.

2.1 Supervised and Self-supervised Pretraining

Supervised and self-supervised pretraining are two prevalent vision representation learning strategies for downstream pathological image analysis [1, 20, 25]. With a supervised learning procedures, ResNet [8] and VGG [22] can be pretrained by ImageNet, which have been widely used in medical image analysis [3, 21]. On the other hand, self-supervised learning (e.g., TransPath [28]) has been increasingly popular for large-scale pathological pretraining. In our JRT method, we employed the ImageNet pretrained ResNet50 and TCGA+PAIP pretrained TransPath as encoders. We directly used the pretrained model weights for the downstream task.

2.2   Joint Representation Tuning

The framework of the proposed JRT is presented in Fig. 1 and 2. The low dimensional features from both supervised and self-supervised models are concatenated to a simple Multi-Layer Perception (MLP) for the downstream survival and diagnosis analyses [10]. To evaluate the representation quality abstracted by a pretrained encoder, we conducted the survival prediction analysis as downstream task. The deep survival loss [30] was used as the loss function. We used Concordance Index (C-Index) [27] as an evaluation metric for our survival prediction. C-Index is defined as the ratio of the predicted survival time in correct order among all uncensored testing samples.

2.3   Evaluate Different Strategies of Using Pretrained Model

We evaluated different ways of utilizing the pretrained models as baselines as shown in Fig. 2. To utilize the pretrained model, there are three basic strategies:

No-freeze. All weights in the pretrained network are freely finetuned using downstream task data. In this case, the pretrained weights are only used as weight initialization.

Encoder-Freeze. The Encoder-freeze strategy freezes the encoder (e.g., convolutional encoder or vision transformer-based encoder) without further changing its weights. Then, the finetuning is only performed on features.

Feature-Direct. Feature-direct strategy is designed as a "two-stage" framework, where the feature encoders are discarded after extracting features. Then the extracted features are directly used for the downstream classification. The advantage of the Feature-direct strategy is that the memory consumption is minimized without using the encoders. However, this strategy is limited by not performing an on-line data augmentation.

3   Experiments

3.1   Data Description

Survival Prediction Task. Two available public datasets were used in this study. The WSI images used for the survival prediction task were from TCGA-GBMLGG [18]. Each image was 1024×1024 resolution. 1505 ROI images from 769 patients were used for prognosis prediction model tuning. ROI patches were curated in [18] from diagnostic slides. We randomly cropped 512×512 image patches from the ROI images.

Classification Task. NCT-CRC-HE [11] from National Center for Tumor Diseases (NCT) was used as the classification dataset (8 colorectal cancer types and normal) with 100,000 images. Images were in size of 224×224 from 86 WSIs.

3.2 Experimental Setting

Our proposed joint finetuning strategy were designed to finetune the model with both CNN features and Transformer features. We used TransPath model [28] and ResNet-50 [5] as the backbones. To fairly evaluate the our joint representation finetuning method, We utilized the same MLP structure as the downstream network for all experiments. The MLP was composed of three fully connected layers. As presented in Fig. 2, the image augmentation could be applied to No-freeze and Encoder-freeze training strategies for both TransPath and ResNet-50. We used Cox Loss [30] for model survival time prediction and Adam optimizer to update MLP. All model training were implemented on NVIDIA P5000 GPU.

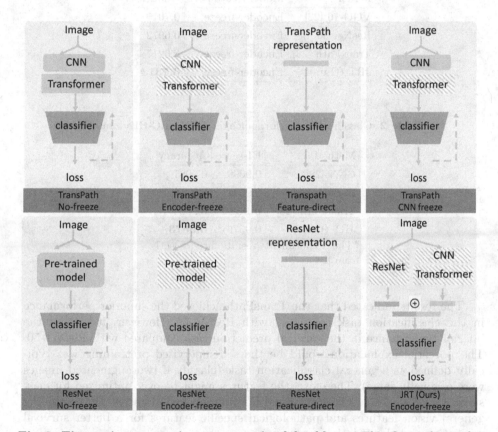

Fig. 2. Finetuning strategies on pretrained backbone. This figure shows the three prevalent finetuning strategies: (1) No-freeze, (2) Encoder-freeze, and (3) Feature-direct using ResNet and TranPath. The highlighted method is the proposed JRT strategy.

4   Results

4.1   Performance on Classification and Survival Prediction

The Table 1 and 2 indicated the performance of the proposed the JRT method as well as the benchmarks in survival prediction and tissue classification tasks. The results indicated that our JRT method achieved superior performance compared with the baseline methods aross two tasks.

Table 1. Survival prediction performance on TCGA-GBMLGG ROI dataset.

Model	Model freeze part	C-index
VGG-16 [22]	Encoder-freeze	0.7010
ResNet-50 [8]	Encoder-freeze	0.6972
TransPath [28]	Encoder-freeze	0.6217
JRT (Ours)	Encoder-freeze	**0.7313**

Table 2. Classification performance on NCT-CRC-HE dataset.

Method	F1-score	Accuracy
CNN [28]*	0.9099	0.9081
ResNet-50 [8]	0.9541	0.9558
TransPath [28]*	**0.9582**	0.9585
JRT (Ours)	0.9576	**0.9673**

*The experiment results are directly from [28].

The results indicated that the TransPath achieved the superior performance in the classification task compared with ResNet-50. However, it yielded the inferior performance in the survival prediction task compared with ResNet-50. The potential explanation would be the self-supervised pretraining was typically defined as a general classification task (classify if two augmented images were originally same). Therefore, the features might be over optimized for classification, while losing essential visual information for prognosis. By combining general vision features and pathological specific features for a better survival prediction and classification performance.

4.2   Computational Resource

Figure 3 presented training speed, C-index performance, and GPU memory consumption for different methods. Note that by using the proposed JRT method, the Feature-direct version (f-JRT) achieved more than 60× training speedup while maintaining 0.707 c-index score compared with non-JRT methods.

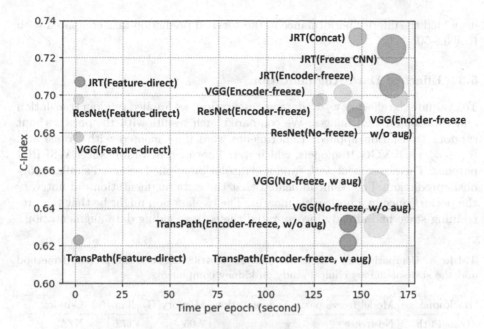

Fig. 3. Visual comparison of different strategies. This figure shows the C-Index versus the model training time required for an epoch. The size of the blobs is proportional to the number of GPU memory consumption.

5 Ablation Studies

The three strategies of using pretrained models were evaluated in the Table 3, including (1) No-freeze, (2) Encoder-free, and (3) Feature-freeze. Since the data augmentation could be applied or not for the No-freeze and Encoder-freeze approaches, we also evaluated the performance of adding data augmentation of downstream finetuning as ablation studies.

5.1 Different Strategies of Using Pretrained Models

From the performance on survival prediction analysis (Table 3), the Encoder-free strategy (with finetuning without updating backbone parameter) achieved similar performance with No-freeze strategy. Thus, the two-stage model yielded the similar performance as the more computational expensive end-to-end training. With two-stage design (Feature-direct), the three single backbone and our JRT method required less GPU memory and training time.

5.2 Effect of Transformer

We compared the transformer based TransPath method with the CNN based ResNet-50 method. The results indicated that the TransPath achieved the superior performance in the classification task compared with ResNet-50. However, it yielded the inferior performance in the survival prediction task compared with ResNet-50.

5.3 Effect of Data Augmentation

To evaluate the effect of w/wo data augmentation, we applied random translation and rotation on ROI images. We compared such results with the ones without random translation applied. Experiments were implemented with TransPath, Resnet-50 and VGG-16 models, which were finetuned by brain cancer WSI ROI patches. The experiment with random translation applied achieved similar prognosis prediction. The result indicated that the data augmentation did not vary the performance in a noticeable margin. The explanation might be that the pretraining stage had already incorporated the corresponding data augmentation.

Table 3. Comparison of volumetric analysis metrics between the proposed method and the state-of-the-art clinical study on kidney components.

Backbone	Model freeze part	Augmentation	Memory(G)	Time(s)	C-index
TransPath	No-freeze	w	7.05	172	N/A
TransPath	No-freeze	w/o	7.05	172	N/A
TransPath	Encoder-freeze	w	2.94	143	0.6318
TransPath	Encoder-freeze	w/o	2.94	143	0.6217
TransPath	CNN part	w/o	6.00	166	0.7050
TransPath	Feature-direct	w/o	1.03	1.74	0.6230
ResNet-50	No-freeze	w	3.28	147	0.6885
ResNet-50	No-freeze	w/o	3.28	147	0.6928
ResNet-50	Encoder-freeze	w	1.32	127	0.6972
ResNet-50	Encoder-freeze	w/o	1.32	129	0.6978
ResNet-50	Feature-direct	w/o	1.05	1.75	0.6977
VGG-16	No-freeze	w	6.32	158	0.6310
VGG-16	No-freeze	w/o	6.32	158	0.6530
VGG-16	Encoder-freeze	w	3.13	140	0.7010
VGG-16	Encoder-freeze	w/o	3.13	144	0.6983
VGG-16	Feature-direct	w/o	1.05	1.75	0.6776
f-JRT (Ours)	Feature-direct	w/o	1.07	2.44	0.7070
JRT (Ours)	TransPath CNN	w	8.331	166	0.7249
JRT (Ours)	Encoder-freeze	w	3.28	148	**0.7313**

"w" in augmentation column means training data are augmented image views. "w/o" means all image views are fed into model without image view augmentation.

6   Conclusion

In this work, we analyze how to leverage the already trained supervised and self-supervised models for pathological survival analysis. We proposed a simple and low-cost JRT representation tuning strategy and shows effective improvement to adapt classification based supervised and self-supervised representation for survival prediction. With the proposed JRT, the Feature-direct finetuning strategy yields 60× training speedup while maintaining superior c-index score compared with non-JRT methods.

References

1. Azizi, S., et al.: Big self-supervised models advance medical image classification. In: Proceedings of the IEEE/CVF International Conference on Computer Vision, pp. 3478–3488 (2021)
2. Bao, H., Dong, L., Wei, F.: Beit: bert pre-training of image transformers. arXiv preprint arXiv:2106.08254 (2021)
3. Bar, Y., Diamant, I., Wolf, L., Greenspan, H.: Deep learning with non-medical training used for chest pathology identification. In: Medical Imaging 2015: Computer-Aided Diagnosis, vol. 9414, p. 94140V. International Society for Optics and Photonics (2015)
4. Bardes, A., Ponce, J., LeCun, Y.: Vicreg: Variance-invariance-covariance regularization for self-supervised learning. arXiv preprint. arXiv:2105.04906 (2021)
5. Chen, R.J., et al.: Pathomic fusion: an integrated framework for fusing histopathology and genomic features for cancer diagnosis and prognosis. IEEE Trans. Med. Imaging **41**, 757–770 (2020)
6. Ciga, O., Xu, T., Martel, A.L.: Self supervised contrastive learning for digital histopathology. Mach. Learn. Appl. **7**, 100198 (2021)
7. David, L., et al.: Applications of deep-learning in exploiting large-scale and heterogeneous compound data in industrial pharmaceutical research. Front. Pharmacol. **10**, 1303 (2019)
8. He, K., Zhang, X., Ren, S., Sun, J.: Deep residual learning for image recognition. In: Proceedings of the IEEE Conference On Computer Vision And Pattern Recognition, pp. 770–778 (2016)
9. Huo, Y., Deng, R., Liu, Q., Fogo, A.B., Yang, H.: AI applications in renal pathology. Kidney Int. **99**(6), 1309–1320 (2021)
10. Jarrett, D., Yoon, J., van der Schaar, M.: Dynamic prediction in clinical survival analysis using temporal convolutional networks. IEEE J. Biomed. Health Inform. **24**(2), 424–436 (2019)
11. Kather, J.N., et al.: Predicting survival from colorectal cancer histology slides using deep learning: a retrospective multicenter study. PLoS Med. **16**(1), e1002730 (2019)
12. Kieffer, B., Babaie, M., Kalra, S., Tizhoosh, H.R.: Convolutional neural networks for histopathology image classification: training vs. using pre-trained networks. In: 2017 Seventh International Conference on Image Processing Theory, Tools and Applications (IPTA), pp. 1–6. IEEE (2017)
13. Kim, Y.J., et al.: PAIP 2019: liver cancer segmentation challenge. Med. Image Anal. **67**, 101854 (2021)

14. Krizhevsky, A., Sutskever, I., Hinton, G.E.: Imagenet classification with deep convolutional neural networks. In: Advances in Neural Information Processing Systems, vol. 25 (2012)
15. Li, R., Yao, J., Zhu, X., Li, Y., Huang, J.: Graph CNN for survival analysis on whole slide pathological images. In: Frangi, A.F., Schnabel, J.A., Davatzikos, C., Alberola-López, C., Fichtinger, G. (eds.) MICCAI 2018. LNCS, vol. 11071, pp. 174–182. Springer, Cham (2018). https://doi.org/10.1007/978-3-030-00934-2_20
16. Liu, Q., et al.: SimTriplet: simple triplet representation learning with a single GPU. In: de Bruijne, M., et al. (eds.) MICCAI 2021. LNCS, vol. 12902, pp. 102–112. Springer, Cham (2021). https://doi.org/10.1007/978-3-030-87196-3_10
17. Lu, Y., Jha, A., Huo, Y.: Contrastive learning meets transfer learning: a case study in medical image analysis. arXiv preprint. arXiv:2103.03166 (2021)
18. Mobadersany, P., et al.: Predicting cancer outcomes from histology and genomics using convolutional networks. Proc. Natl. Acad. Sci. **115**(13), E2970–E2979 (2018)
19. Mormont, R., Geurts, P., Marée, R.: Multi-task pre-training of deep neural networks for digital pathology. IEEE J. Biomed. Health Inform. **25**(2), 412–421 (2020)
20. Peikari, M., Salama, S., Nofech-Mozes, S., Martel, A.L.: A cluster-then-label semi-supervised learning approach for pathology image classification. Sci. Rep. **8**(1), 1–13 (2018)
21. Rai, T., et al.: Can imagenet feature maps be applied to small histopathological datasets for the classification of breast cancer metastatic tissue in whole slide images?. In: Medical Imaging 2019: Digital Pathology, vol. 10956, pp. 191–200. SPIE (2019)
22. Simonyan, K., Zisserman, A.: Very deep convolutional networks for large-scale image recognition (2015)
23. Tang, B., Li, A., Li, B., Wang, M.: Capsurv: capsule network for survival analysis with whole slide pathological images. IEEE Access **7**, 26022–26030 (2019)
24. Tellez, D., van der Laak, J., Ciompi, F.: Gigapixel whole-slide image classification using unsupervised image compression and contrastive training (2018)
25. Thongprayoon, C., et al.: Promises of big data and artificial intelligence in nephrology and transplantation (2020)
26. Tomczak, K., Czerwińska, P., Wiznerowicz, M.: The cancer genome atlas (TCGA): an immeasurable source of knowledge. Contemp. Oncol. **19**(1A), A68 (2015)
27. Uno, H., Cai, T., Pencina, M.J., D'Agostino, R.B., Wei, L.J.: On the c-statistics for evaluating overall adequacy of risk prediction procedures with censored survival data. Stat. Med. **30**(10), 1105–1117 (2011)
28. Wang, X., et al.: TransPath: transformer-based self-supervised learning for histopathological image classification. In: de Bruijne, M., et al. (eds.) MICCAI 2021. LNCS, vol. 12908, pp. 186–195. Springer, Cham (2021). https://doi.org/10.1007/978-3-030-87237-3_18
29. Yang, P., Hong, Z., Yin, X., Zhu, C., Jiang, R.: Self-supervised visual representation learning for histopathological images. In: de Bruijne, M., et al. (eds.) MICCAI 2021. LNCS, vol. 12902, pp. 47–57. Springer, Cham (2021). https://doi.org/10.1007/978-3-030-87196-3_5
30. Yao, J., Zhu, X., Jonnagaddala, J., Hawkins, N., Huang, J.: Whole slide images based cancer survival prediction using attention guided deep multiple instance learning networks. Med. Image Anal. **65**, 101789 (2020)
31. Zhu, X., Yao, J., Huang, J.: Deep convolutional neural network for survival analysis with pathological images. In: 2016 IEEE International Conference on Bioinformatics and Biomedicine (BIBM), pp. 544–547. IEEE (2016)

Pathological Image Contrastive Self-supervised Learning

Wenkang Qin[1], Shan Jiang[2], and Lin Luo[1,3(✉)]

[1] College of Engineering, Peking University, Beijing, China
[2] Beijing Institute of Collaborative Innovation, Beijing, China
[3] Southern University of Science and Technology, Shenzhen, China
luol@pku.edu.cn

Abstract. Self-supervised learning methods have been receiving wide attentions in recent years, where contrastive learning starts to show encouraging performance in many tasks in the field of computer vision. Contrastive learning methods build pre-training weight parameters by crafting positive/negative samples and optimizing their distance in the feature space. It is easy to construct positive/negative samples on natural images, but the methods cannot directly apply to histopathological images because of the unique characteristics of the images such as staining invariance and vertical flip invariance. This paper proposes a general method for constructing clinical-equivalent positive sample pairs on histopathological images for applying contrastive learning on histopathological images. Results on the PatchCamelyon benchmark show that our method can improve model accuracy up to 6% while reducing the training costs, as well as reducing reliance on labeled data.

Keywords: Histopathological images · Self-supervised learning · Representation learning

1 Introduction

The rapid development of deep learning in computer vision have driven the wide applications in the field of medical images, but the high cost of expert labeling for medical images leads to the shortage of mass labeled data. Self-supervised learning is proposed in NLP to solve labeling issue as an unsupervised pre-training strategy using a formulated pretext task on unlabeled data Handcrafted pretext tasks include solving jigsaw puzzles [15], relative patch prediction [8] and colorization [22]. However, many of these tasks rely on ad-hoc heuristics that could limit the generalization and transferability of learned representations for downstream tasks.

Contrastive learning [3,5,9,11,20] has emerged as the front-runner for self-supervision and has demonstrated superior performance on downstream tasks. Contrastive learning of visual representations make full utilizes unlabeled data

X. Xu et al. (Eds.): REMIA 2022, LNCS 13543, pp. 85–94, 2022.
https://doi.org/10.1007/978-3-031-16876-5_9

for deep model training by generating a pretrained weight with intrinsic feature representation on unlabeled data and further fine-tuning it on downstream tasks. All contrastive learning frameworks such as Momentum Contrast (MoCo) [4,6,11] involve maximizing consistency between positive examples through a contrastive loss function, which is a pretraining paradigm to force the models to learn the intrinsic representations. The key of the paradigm is how to construct the positive sample pair, that is, what kind of samples are regarded as the same instance in the feature space. Several methods [3,5,9,11,20] have achieved promising gains on natural images with pair construction methods (cutting, scaling, horizontal flipping, color jitter, etc.). However, the underlining hypotheses of data distribution variance and in-variance for medical images have different characteristics thus more explorations are needed to extend these methods into medical image cases [2,17].

Diagnosis on Histopathological images is the golden standard for cancer diagnosis [19] and molecular feature prediction. It also suffers from the lack of mass data with expert labelling to learn with histopathological images. Therefore, how to use unlabeled data to learn an effective feature representation is important. Histopathological images are produced through physical and digital process involving specimen fixing, sectioning, staining, slide sealing, and digital scanning, etc. It is obvious that image direction has no meaning because specimens can be placed randomly on the glass slides, thus vertical flipping, which is not regarded as positive case for natural image, can be used as positive case for histopathological images. Moreover, color channels from hematoxylin-eosin staining are meaningful for doctors to diagnose, so the color jitter in constructing positive case needs to be carefully designed to be practical to real clinic use. In this paper, we propose a method for constructing positive sample pairs utilizing the unique clinical characteristics of histopathological images, in order to extend the contrastive learning framework from natural images to histopathological images, especially in classification tasks.

We first analyze three important properties of histopathological images, namely, staining invariance, geometric invariance, and scale uniqueness. Stain invariance means that two histopathological images with different staining appearances have the same semantics. Geometric invariance refers to horizontal inversion invariance, vertical inversion invariance and rotation invariance in histopathological images, which is different from natural images, which often only have horizontal inversion invariance. Scale uniqueness means that histopathological images at different scales have semantic differences. From these properties, we propose some transformations for histopathological images and form them into a pipeline for constructing positive sample pairs for histopathological images.

We integrate the proposed methods with the MoCov2 framework [4] and evaluate both on PatchCamelyon [19]. Two evaluation protocols, linear prob and finetune, are used for evaluation. Experimental results show that our method effectively reduces the training cost and improves the model with less labeled data. e.g. with only 5% of labeled data and less training time, our method raises the accuracy up to 6% and even outperforms the fully supervised learning. The main contribution of our paper is to propose a contrastive learning sample enhancement method specifically for histopathological images, and propose a staining perturbation method to simulate the possible staining shift in histopathological images.

2   Revisiting Contrastive Learning

Contrastive learning is a class of pre-training methods that employ unlabeled data for self-supervised training to obtain good feature representations. It has been extensively studied in the field of computer vision [3]. However, most of these methods [3,5,9,11,20] are studied and experimented on natural images, and their application to histopathological images is limited. In the contrastive learning method, a training sample first undergoes a series of image transformations to form different views. Different views of the same image are considered an instance.

During training, through a specific loss function such as InfoNCE [3], the distance of the same instance in the feature space is shortened, and the distance of different instances in the feature space is pulled away. Given an anchor random variable $x_{1,i} \sim p(x_1)$, the popular contrastive learning framework aims to differentiate a positive sample $x_{2,i} \sim p(x_2|x_{1,i})$ from negative samples $x_{2,j} \sim p(x_2)$. This is usually done by minimizing the InfoNCE loss [13]:

$$\mathcal{L}_{\text{NCE}} = -\mathbb{E}\left[\log\frac{f(x_{2,i}, x_{1,i})}{\sum_{j=1}^{N} f(x_{2,j}, x_{1,i})}\right] \tag{1}$$

where $f(x_{2,j}, x_{1,i})$ is a positive scoring function usually chosen as a log-bilinear model. It has been shown that minimizing $\mathcal{L}_{\text{NCE}}$ is equivalent to maximizing a lower bound of the mutual information $I(x_2; x_1)$. Many negative samples are required to properly approximate the negative distribution $p(x_2)$ and tighten the lower bound.

In this process, the most critical problem is how to construct different instances of the same training sample. Because histopathological images and natural images have many different properties, such as staining invariance. By designing reasonable histopathological image transformations, we can well apply the contrastive learning method to histopathological image-related tasks [1,19].

Therefore, our work remains under the framework of contrastive learning. Our goal is to tune the sample augmentation part of the contrastive learning framework so that it can fully exploit the properties of histopathological images so that feature invariance can be learned during the self-supervised pre-training stage.

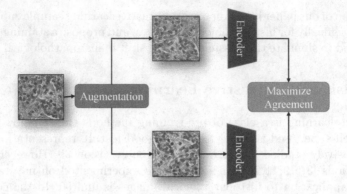

Fig. 1. Contrastive learning frameworks. After the input image is augmented, its feature representation is obtained through the encoder, and then the distance between the positive samples in the feature space is shortened to obtain a better feature representation.

3   Histopathological Contrastive Learning

In this section, we will start from the properties of histopathological images and elicit the image transformations required for self-supervised training of pathological images. We introduce our proposed staining perturbation method to perturb the staining of histopathological images so that the network can better learn staining invariance. Finally, we describe how we combine these transformations to form a pipeline of histopathological image transformations.

3.1   Properties of Histopathological Images

Among histopathological images, there are some peculiar properties that do not exist in natural images, or are different from natural images. Here, we believe that in the process of model training, the feature space should have the following three important properties:

Staining Invariance. In the process of making histopathological images, due to different standards used in different hospitals and data centers, different dyeing agents, different operators, and different scanners, etc., the final digital pathological image will appear different in appearance. Usually, in the process of training, preprocessing such as staining normalization is performed on the histopathological image, so that the color distribution of the pathological image is as consistent as possible. But no matter how the same pathological image is stained, it should be regarded as the same instance without losing features. That is, histopathological images should have staining invariance.

Geometric Invariance. In histopathological images, when the tissue is rotated or flipped to different perspectives, the resulting feature representation should also be invariant. This is because the organization itself is not directional. Therefore, in the process of self-supervised training, for the same training sample, after horizontal flipping, vertical flipping or rotation, it should be regarded as the same instance. Technically, due to the use of patches for training, some information may be lost when rotating at any angle, so we only rotate by an integer multiple of 90°. Since the histopathological pictures may be out of focus, images with different out-of-focus should be regarded as the same instance.

Scale Uniqueness. In the transformation of natural images, different cropping and scaling of the same image are usually regarded as the same instance. In tasks related to histopathological images, usually regardless of the single-scale model or the multi-scale model, the scale of the input histopathological image is deterministic and unique. Images at different zoom ratios and images at different resolutions should have different semantics. Therefore, in the fully-supervised training stage, we do not perform cropping and scaling transformations to ensure that the features have scale uniqueness. But we found that it's helpful when cropping and scaling in self-supervised training stage. So crop and scale are applied in the self-supervised stage.

3.2 Stain Perturbation

In order to realize the transformation of the staining, we adopt the staining perturbation method. This method is derived from the color deconvolution method [16]. This method first needs to obtain the optical density representation of the histopathological image. The optical density representation and the light intensity have the following relationship:

$$OD = -log(I) \tag{2}$$

where I represents the light intensity representation of the pathological image, and OD represents the optical density representation. In the optical density space, the representation of HE-stained pathological images can be obtained by the linear combination of two color feature vectors. That is, OD can be decomposed into the following representation:

$$OD = S \times C \tag{3}$$

where S is a 2×3-dimensional matrix, representing the staining feature vector, and C is the staining concentration of each pixel. There are many ways to get the result of this decomposition, for example [14,18], here we use the [14] method. After getting this representation, we add a noise δ to S sampled from a Gaussian distribution with mean 0 and variance 0.1. The optical density space of the final perturbed histopathological image is expressed as:

$$OD_{Pert} = (S + \delta) \times C \tag{4}$$

where OD_{Pert} represents the perturbed histopathological image. The specific perturbation implementation can refer to the appendix.

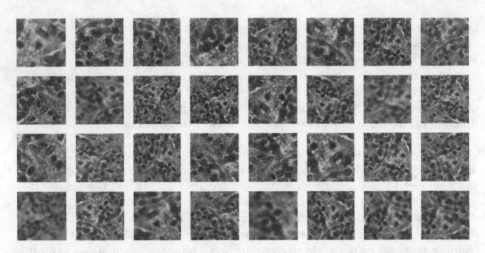

Fig. 2. Some samples after pipeline processing. These images are all regarded as the same instance and are regarded as positive examples during the training process. All transformations in the pipeline are random and can form a large number of pairs of positive samples.

3.3 Pipeline of Transforms

To make the feature space satisfy color invariance, we use the color perturbation method described above to construct instances. Special, sometimes due to the deterioration of the dye, the final histopathological image is extremely distorted. In order to simulate this situation, we add random grayscale images to perform extreme disturbances. We used random Gaussian blur to simply simulate possible out-of-focus situations. To achieve geometric invariance, we add random horizontal flips, random vertical flips, and random rotations to the transformation pipeline. But we only rotate by an integer multiple of 90°. We use random cropping and scaling to keep the scale unique in pre-train stage. But it will be canceled when finetune stage. All the above transformations constitute our pipeline for self-supervised pretraining. The final augmentation result is shown in Fig. 2.

4   Experiments

Our experiments were performed on PatchCamelyon [1,19]. MoCov2 [4] is selected for the contrastive learning framework. At the same time, we use two benchmarks for evaluation. The linear prob evaluation protocol, which freezes all convolutional layers and trains only the last linear layers, was widely adopted in previous work [3,9,11] on contrastive learning, but now suffers from some criticism [10]. The finetune evaluation protocol, which does not freeze the convolutional layers, but fine-tunes all layers, is also widely adopted and considered more suitable for evaluating the effect of pre-training than the linear prob. We detail the dataset we adopted and the results of the evaluation in this chapter.

4.1   Dataset

We evaluate our method on PatchCamelyon benchmark [1,19]. The PatchCamelyon benchmark is an image classification dataset. It consists of 327,680 color
images (96 × 96px) extracted from histopathologic scans of lymph node sections.
Each image is annoted with a binary label indicating presence of metastatic tissue. For semi-supervised training evaluation, we divided the training set into
1%, 5%, 10% and 30% data sets according to the stratified sampling method.

4.2   Implementation Details

Our codebase is mainly based on mmselfsup [7], which is an open source self-
supervised representation learning toolbox based on PyTorch. For the simplicity
of the experiment, we choose Resnet-18 [12] as the backbone network. We use
MoCo [4] for the contrastive learning framework. These works have been proven
effective and widely adopted. We use the [14] method to deconvolute the coloration to obtain the colorization vector of the image, and apply a perturbation.
Here our perturbed noise is sampled from a Gaussian distribution with mean
0 and variance 0.1 [21]. In the pre-training phase, we use 2 Nvidia Tesla V100
GPUs. The batch size on each GPU is 64. During training we set the weight
decay to 0, and the learning rate to $1e-4$ with a learning rate of 0.03 and a
momentum of 0.9. We train for 200 epochs and use the results from the last
epochs.

After pre-training, we evaluate the results using two widely adopted evaluation protocols in the field of image self-supervised learning, linear prob and
finetune. When using the linear prob evaluation protocol, the pre-trained convolutional layers are all frozen, and we set the weight decay and learning rate to
different values for training the linear layer after the convolutional layer. In this
setting we only train for 1 epoch on the supervised dataset and report the final
results on the test set. When evaluating the protocol using finetune, we set the
weight decay to $1e-4$, the learning rate to 0.01, and train the entire network for
5 epochs. In the semi-supervised setting, we use the above parameters to train
with 5% – 30% labeled data.

4.3   Results

Under the finetune protocol, we tested the performance of training 1 epoch with
different learning rates and weight decay. The result is shown in the Table 1.
It is obvious from the table that after pre-training, we only train one linear
layer and can get better performance than supervised learning, up to about
5% improvement. This demonstrates the effectiveness of feature representations
pretrained by contrastive learning with our transformation method.

Table 1. Finetune linear layers on pretrained weights. We first get an initialization weight by self-supervised training, then freeze all convolutional layers, and train a linear layer for classification after the convolutional layers. This evaluation method is widely used in natural images, but it has also been criticized. To be fair, we still use this evaluation method. HCL denotes our histopathological contrastive learning method. Possibly due to too few samples for fine-tuning, experimental results show that fine-tuning with more epochs may lead to model degradation.

Methdos	Learning rate	Weight decay	Epochs	Accuracy(%)
Baseline [12]	0.01	1e−4	10	81.94
Imagenet-pretrained	0.01	1e−4	10	82.13
MoCo [4] (finetune)	0.01	1e−4	10	81.47
HCL (finetune)	0.01	0	1	86.61
HCL (finetune)	0.01	1e−4	1	87.05
HCL (finetune)	0.01	1e−3	1	85.94
HCL (finetune)	0.001	0	1	86.78
HCL (finetune)	0.001	1e−4	1	86.78
HCL (finetune)	0.001	1e−3	1	86.92

In the semi-supervised setting, our experiments with different data scales are shown in the Table 2. We can clearly observe from the results that, after pre-training with contrastive learning of our feature transformations, we can achieve significantly higher performance than models trained on the supervised full training set using only 5% of the labeled data.

Table 2. Fine-tuning experiments in a semi-supervised setting. We performed self-supervised pre-training on the full unlabeled training set, and then used only part of the labeled training set in the fine-tuning process. As can be seen from the results, without freezing the convolutional layers, we achieved 88% correct classification with only 5% of the data, which is 6% higher than training with 100% of the supervised data.

Experiments	Data ratio(%)	Amount	Weight decay	Epochs	Accuracy
Fully-supervised	–	262144	1e−4	10	81.94
Semi (linear)	1%	2621	0	10	72.94
Semi (linear)	5%	13106	0	10	78.67
Semi (linear)	10%	26214	0	10	80.23
Semi (linear)	30%	78642	0	10	81.92
Semi (linear)	100%	262144	0	10	86.60
Semi (finetune)	1%	2621	1e−4	5	86.01
Semi (finetune)	5%	13106	1e−4	5	88.33
Semi (finetune)	10%	26214	1e−4	5	86.91

The above experimental results show that after our model pre-training:

1. It can speed up the convergence speed of the model: after the pre-training is completed, we only need to train 1 epoch to achieve better performance than 10 epochs of fully supervised training;
2. Better performance can be achieved: whether under the linear prob protocol or the finetune protocol, the performance after pre-training is significantly better than that of full-supervised training;
3. The reliance on data annotation can be reduced: After self-supervised training with our method, even with only 5% of the data, it can achieve better performance than the full supervision of 100% of the data.

These results fully demonstrate the effectiveness of applying our method to a contrastive learning framework, which may reduce the training cost while improving performance on tasks related to histopathological images.

5   Conclusion

In this paper, we summarize the different properties of histopathological image-related tasks and natural image-related tasks. Based on these properties, we propose image transformations for self-supervised pre-training of histopathological images. We build on this approach with self-supervised training using MoCo [4]. Both fully-supervised and semi-supervised linear prob and finetune evaluations are tested on pretrained weights. Experimental results show that our method can effectively learn representations of histopathological images. And in semi-supervised evaluation, we can achieve better results than full supervision with only 5% of the data, while lowering the training cost.

Acknowledgements. This research was supported in part by the Foundation of Shenzhen Science and Technology Innovation Committee (JCYJ20180507181527806).

References

1. Bejnordi, B.E., et al.: Diagnostic assessment of deep learning algorithms for detection of lymph node metastases in women with breast cancer. Jama **318**(22), 2199–2210 (2017)
2. Chaitanya, K., Erdil, E., Karani, N., Konukoglu, E.: Contrastive learning of global and local features for medical image segmentation with limited annotations. arXiv: Computer. Vision and Pattern Recognition (2020)
3. Chen, T., Kornblith, S., Norouzi, M., Hinton, G.: A simple framework for contrastive learning of visual representations. In: International Conference on Machine Learning, pp. 1597–1607. PMLR (2020)
4. Chen, X., Fan, H., Girshick, R., He, K.: Improved baselines with momentum contrastive learning. arXiv preprint. arXiv:2003.04297 (2020)
5. Chen, X., He, K.: Exploring simple siamese representation learning. In: Proceedings of the IEEE/CVF Conference on Computer Vision and Pattern Recognition, pp. 15750–15758 (2021)

6. Chen, X., Xie, S., He, K.: An empirical study of training self-supervised vision transformers. In: Proceedings of the IEEE/CVF International Conference on Computer Vision, pp. 9640–9649 (2021)
7. Contributors, M.: MMSelfSup: Openmmlab self-supervised learning toolbox and benchmark. https://github.com/open-mmlab/mmselfsup (2021)
8. Doersch, C., Gupta, A., Efros, A.A.: Unsupervised visual representation learning by context prediction. In: International Conference on Computer Vision (2015)
9. Grill, J.B., et al.: Bootstrap your own latent-a new approach to self-supervised learning. In: Advances in Neural Information Processing Systems, vol. 33, pp. 21271–21284 (2020)
10. He, K., Chen, X., Xie, S., Li, Y., Dollár, P., Girshick, R.: Masked autoencoders are scalable vision learners (2021)
11. He, K., Fan, H., Wu, Y., Xie, S., Girshick, R.: Momentum contrast for unsupervised visual representation learning. In: Proceedings of the IEEE/CVF Conference on Computer Vision and Pattern Recognition, pp. 9729–9738 (2020)
12. He, K., Zhang, X., Ren, S., Sun, J.: Deep residual learning for image recognition. In: Proceedings of the IEEE Conference on Computer Vision and Pattern Recognition, pp. 770–778 (2016)
13. Li, Z., Chen, Z., Li, A., Fang, L., Jiang, Q., Liu, X., Jiang, J., Zhou, B., Zhao, H.: SimIPU: simple 2d image and 3d point cloud unsupervised pre-training for spatial-aware visual representations (2021)
14. Macenko, M., et al.: A method for normalizing histology slides for quantitative analysis. In: 2009 IEEE International Symposium on Biomedical Imaging: From Nano to Macro, pp. 1107–1110. IEEE (2009)
15. Noroozi, M., Favaro, P.: Unsupervised learning of visual representations by solving jigsaw puzzles. In: Leibe, B., Matas, J., Sebe, N., Welling, M. (eds.) ECCV 2016. LNCS, vol. 9910, pp. 69–84. Springer, Cham (2016). https://doi.org/10.1007/978-3-319-46466-4_5
16. Ruifrok, A.C., Johnston, D.A., et al.: Quantification of histochemical staining by color deconvolution. Anal. Quant. Cytol. Histol. 23(4), 291–299 (2001)
17. Sowrirajan, H., Yang, J., Ng, A.Y., Rajpurkar, P.: Moco-cxr: Moco pretraining improves representation and transferability of chest x-ray models. arXiv : Computer Vision and Pattern Recognition (2020)
18. Vahadane, A., et al.: Structure-preserving color normalization and sparse stain separation for histological images. IEEE Trans. Med. Imaging 35(8), 1962–1971 (2016)
19. Veeling, B.S., Linmans, J., Winkens, J., Cohen, T., Welling, M.: Rotation equivariant CNNs for digital pathology. In: Frangi, A.F., Schnabel, J.A., Davatzikos, C., Alberola-López, C., Fichtinger, G. (eds.) MICCAI 2018. LNCS, vol. 11071, pp. 210–218. Springer, Cham (2018). https://doi.org/10.1007/978-3-030-00934-2_24
20. Wu, Z., Xiong, Y., Yu, S.X., Lin, D.: Unsupervised feature learning via non-parametric instance discrimination. In: Proceedings of the IEEE conference on computer vision and pattern recognition, pp. 3733–3742 (2018)
21. Yang, P., Hong, Z., Yin, X., Zhu, C., Jiang, R.: Self-supervised visual representation learning for histopathological images. In: de Bruijne, M., et al. (eds.) MICCAI 2021. LNCS, vol. 12902, pp. 47–57. Springer, Cham (2021). https://doi.org/10.1007/978-3-030-87196-3_5
22. Zhang, R., Isola, P., Efros, A.A.: Colorful image colorization. arXiv: Computer. Vision and Pattern Recognition (2016)

Investigation of Training Multiple Instance Learning Networks with Instance Sampling

Aliasghar Tarkhan[1]([✉]), Trung Kien Nguyen[2], Noah Simon[1], and Jian Dai[2]

[1] Department of Bioststistics, University of Washington, Seattle, USA
{atarkhan,nrsimon}@uw.edu
[2] PHC Imaging Group, Genenetch, South San Francisco, USA
{nguyenk8,daij12}@gene.com

Abstract. One challenge of training deep neural networks with gigapixel whole-slide images (WSIs) is the lack of annotation at pixel level or patch (instance) level due to the high cost and time-consuming labeling effort. Multiple instance learning (MIL) as a typical weakly supervised learning method aimed to resolve this challenge by using only the slide-level label without needing patch labels. Not all patches/instances are predictive of the outcome. The attention-based MIL method leverages this fact to enhance the performance by weighting the instances based on their contribution to predicting the outcome. A WSI typically contains hundreds of thousands of image patches. Training a deep neural network with thousands of image patches per slide is computationally expensive and requires a lot of time for convergence. One way to alleviate this issue is to sample a subset of instances/patches from the available instances within each bag for training. While the benefit of sampling strategies for decreasing computing time might be evident, there is a lack of effort to investigate their performances. This project proposes and compares an adaptive sampling strategy with other sampling strategies. Although all sampling strategies substantially reduce computation time, their performance is influenced by the number of selected instances. We show that if we are limited to only select a few instances (e.g., in order of 1~10 instances), the adaptive sampling outperforms other sampling strategies. However, if we are allowed to select more instances (e.g., in order of 100~1000 instances), the random sampling outperforms other sampling strategies.

Keywords: Attention · Computational pathology · Deep learning · Multiple instance learning · Prostate cancer · Sampling · Transfer learning · Weekly supervised learning · Second keyword

1 Introduction

Using high-resolution Whole-Slide Images (WSIs) from biopsies has become the gold standard for diagnosing many diseases, such as prostate cancer [1–3]. How-

Genentech Personalized Healthcare Digital Pathology Program.

ever, the manual inspection of the entire WSI by an expert is costly and time-consuming, and it is prone to the observer variability issue [4]. The goal of computational pathology is to build automated tools to analyze gigapixel WSIs and save time and cost while providing high-quality health care [5,6]. Developing such automated tools by training the deep neural networks is challenging: WSIs are gigapixel images and are too big to be fed into the neural networks. A WSI may be divided into numerous smaller regions (usually hundreds of thousands of images with size, e.g., 256×256), called patches or tiles. The challenge of training a deep neural network with these small images is the lack of pixel-level annotation: labels are only provided at the slide (patient) level. Annotating these image regions (patches) is costly (labor and time) [7].

Multiple instance learning (MIL), as a typical weakly supervised learning method [8,9] tackles this challenge by training the neural networks using only the bag-level labels. However, the upcoming challenge with the MIL problem is that not all instances (image tiles) are equally predictive of the bag label (class), and some of them may even relate to the other classes [10]. Some works considered combining the instance-level responses from a classifier to alleviate this challenge [11–13]. Among them, [13] proposed an attention-based deep MIL framework to deal with this challenge. Their proposed framework includes (1) an attention network and (2) a classification network. These two networks are trained simultaneously. The attention network has parameters for updating the attention (importance) weights of different instances, while the classification network has parameters for the classification task. But there is still a challenge: They use all instances per bag across all training iterates. A WSI has hundreds of thousands of image tiles, and training a neural network with these instances is time-consuming and computationally expensive. An attention MIL network may not need to be trained by noisy or less-predictive instances.

This paper investigates different sampling strategies for training the attention-based deep MIL framework: (1) no sampling, (2) random sampling, (3) adaptive sampling, and (4) top-k sampling. We show how the sampling strategies substantially reduce computation time. We also show that a random sampling strategy can improve performance compared to no sampling (i.e., using whole instances in the original work [13]) if we choose enough instances.

2   MIL and Attention-Based MIL Networks

2.1   MIL Problem Formulation

Suppose there are N subjects (or patients) with bags of images $\mathcal{X}^{(1)}, \mathcal{X}^{(2)}, \ldots,$ $\mathcal{X}^{(N)}$ and bag-level binary labels $y^{(1)}, y^{(2)}, \ldots, y^{(N)} \in \{0, 1, \ldots, C-1\}$ where C is number of classes. The bag for n-th patient (i.e., $\mathcal{X}^{(n)}$) contains K_n instance images $X_1^{(n)}, X_2^{(n)}, \ldots, X_{K_n}^{(n)}$. In classical supervised learning, we have $K_n = 1$ image per subject with label $y^{(n)}$. To decrease computing time and cost, it is common to use a state-of-the-art pre-trained network such as *ResNet50* [14] to extract a low-dimensional embedding feature $h_k^{(n)}$ from k^{th} instance image. After that, we have dataset $\{(\boldsymbol{h}_k^{(n)}, y^{(n)}), \text{ for } n = 1, 2, \ldots N \text{ and } k = 1, 2, \ldots, K_n\}$. The goal of MIL problem is to train a neural network using the bag label $y^{(n)}$ and embedding features $\boldsymbol{h}_k^{(n)}$, $k = 1, 2, \ldots, K_n$. For binary classification task (i.e., $C = 2$), the basic assumption of a MIL problem is:

$$y^{(n)} = \begin{cases} 0, & \text{iff } \sum_{k=1}^{K_n} y_k^{(n)} = 0 \\ 1, & \text{otherwise.} \end{cases} \tag{1}$$

which is undesirable from an optimization standpoint. An alternative is to pool instances (e.g., by using element-wise maximum or average operators) to get a single aggregated feature representing each bag. Such pooling approaches are generally pre-calculated and not trainable.

2.2 Attention-Based MIL

Attention-based MIL [13] resolves this issue by using a combined architecture of two trainable networks: an attention network and a classification network. The attention network aggregates the embedding features as

$$\boldsymbol{h}_{bag}^{(n)} = \sum_{k=1}^{K_n} a_k^{(n)} \boldsymbol{h}_k^{(n)},$$

$$a_k^{(n)} = \frac{exp\{\boldsymbol{w}^T (tanh(\boldsymbol{V}\boldsymbol{h}_k^{(n)}) \odot sigm(\boldsymbol{U}\boldsymbol{h}_k^{(n)}))\}}{\sum_{k'=1}^{K_n} exp\{\boldsymbol{w}(tanh(\boldsymbol{V}\boldsymbol{h}_{k'}^{(n)}) \odot sigm(\boldsymbol{U}\boldsymbol{h}_{k'}^{(n)}))))\}}, \tag{2}$$

where $\boldsymbol{w} \in \mathbb{R}^{L \times 1}, \boldsymbol{U} \in \mathbb{R}^{L \times M}$, and $\boldsymbol{V} \in \mathbb{R}^{L \times M}$ are trainable parameters included in the attention network; $tanh(.)$ and $sigm(.)$ are the element-wise hyperbolic tangent and sigmoid functions; $\odot$ is an element-wise multiplication. Such a MIL pooling mechanism preserves flexibility and interpretability (see Sect. 2.4 in [13]). The classification network receives (2) as its input and calculates a $C \times 1$ vector of class prediction scores as

$$\boldsymbol{s}_{bag}^{(n)} = \boldsymbol{W}_c^T \boldsymbol{h}_{bag}^{(n)}, \tag{3}$$

Finally, one can estimate the bag class by

$$\widehat{y}^{(n)} = \arg\max_c \{\boldsymbol{s}_{bag}^{(n)}\}. \tag{4}$$

In many pathology applications, many instances within each WSI might increase computing time and cost. The following section presents different sampling strategies to overcome these possible shortcomings.

3 Sampling Strategies for Attention-Based MIL

3.1 Random Sampling

With a random sampling strategy, we randomly draw a limited number of instances (or images) to train the deep neural network. This strategy has been used in the literature [15–17] and showed great success in reducing computing resources and time. However, there is a lack of investigation on the computing time and performance of random sampling in the deep attention-based MIL network.

3.2   Adaptive Sampling

In practice (e.g., for prostate cancer [3]), many instance images may not contribute to the class of a bag (patient). Some previous works have aimed at this issue [18–20]; however, they used all instances in each bag. We propose an adaptive sampling strategy to draw G instances per bag that we believe are particularly informative for identifying the class. These instances are identified by constructing a sampling distribution: For the nth patient, we construct the sampling distribution as a multi-nominal distribution with the vector of probabilities $\mathcal{P}^{(n)} = (p_1^{(n)} = a_1^{(n)}, p_2^{(n)} = a_2^{(n)}, \ldots, p_{K_n}^{(n)} = a_{K_n}^{(n)}), 0 \leq p_k^{(n)} \leq 1, \sum_{k=1}^{K_n} p_k^{(n)} = 1$ where $a_k^{(n)}$ is the attention weight for kth instance of nth patient, extracted from a forward attention network given by (2). We propose to draw a subset of G indices from the sampling distribution $\mathcal{P}^{(n)}$ as

$$(I_1^{(n)}, I_2^{(n)}, \ldots, I_G^{(n)}) \sim \mathcal{P}^{(n)}. \tag{5}$$

Following (5), instances with higher attention weights (i.e., higher $a_k^{(n)}$) will be selected more often for the next training iteration (epoch). After that, we train the attention-based neural network following (2) to (4) but only using the G selected instances instead of using all K_n available instances ($G << K_n$). Since the network parameters' estimates and the attention weights $a_k^{(n)}$ are initially noisier, we include a few initial warm-up iterations for which we use all K_n instances to train the neural network. Furthermore, to save computing time/resources, one might decide to estimate $\mathcal{P}^{(n)}$ on every e_{update} epochs instead of on every single epoch.

Note that authors in [21] compared uniform and adaptive instance sampling strategies with those without sampling. But they fixed the attention network for the uniform sampling. We take a more fair approach and consider the same network architecture for all strategies we aim to compare in this paper. We also extended the work in [22] by exploring more methods, datasets, and a broader range for the number of selected instances G.

3.3   Top-k Sampling

Top-k sampling strategy has been used in the computational pathology literature [23,24]. This sampling strategy selects the top k instances with the highest instance-level score and then trains the neural network. This paper selects top-k instances with the highest attention weights given by (2). Figure 1 illustrates different instance sampling strategies.

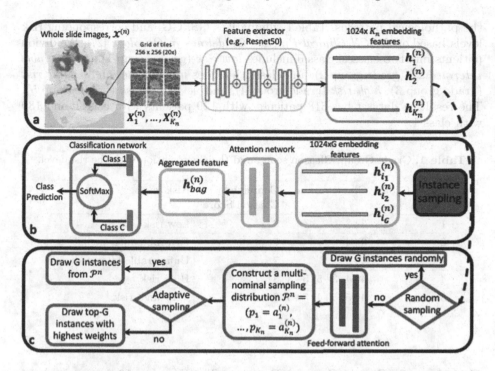

Fig. 1. Different instance sampling strategies. a: pre-processing We sample patches from the WSI $X^{(n)}$ and use pre-trained network (e.g., ResNet50) to extract lower-dimensional features $h_1^{(n)}$, ..., $h_{K_n}^{(n)}$. **b: training procedure** We use a subset of G instances (selected by strategies in panel **c**) and obtain aggregated feature $h_{bag}^{(n)}$ using the attention network. Then, we predict the class label using the classification network. **c: instance sampling strategies** We use the trained (fixed) feed-forward attention network to estimate the sampling distribution $\mathcal{P}^{(n)}$ and then draw G instances out of K_n instances using different sampling strategies.

4 Dataset, Network Architecures, and Tuning Hyper-parameters

4.1 Datasets

For all datasets used in this paper, we followed the pre-procedure used in [18] to sample tiles from WSIs and extract 1024×1 embedding features using [14].

TCGA-PRAD (Prostate Cancer) Dataset. The Cancer Genome Atlas (TCGA) repository of prostate adenocarcinoma (TCGA-PRAD) dataset [25] to evaluate our proposed approach. The Gleason score (GS) from the biopsied tissue is the common method to measure the cancer status [26]. The GS is the sum of primary and secondary scores, ranging from 3 to 5. As an alternative, Grade Group (GG) divides prostates cancer patients into five groups based on the pathological patterns. Table 1 summarizes GS, GG, and corresponding risk levels based on *NCCN Clinical Practice Guidelines in Oncology* [27]. We divide patients into two classes: class 0 includes *low risk* (grade group 1) and *favorable intermediate* (grade group 2); and class 1 includes *unfavorable intermediate risk* (grade group 3), *high risk* (grade group 4), and *very high risk* (grade group 5). The resulting dataset has 318 patients, with 129 patients with class 0 and 189 with class 1.

Table 1. Grade Group, Gleason score, and their association with the risk level.

Grade Group	Gleason score	Combined Gleason Score	Risk level
1	3+3	6	Low risk
2	3+4	7	Favorable intermediate
3	4+3	7	Unfavorable intermediate
4	4+4, 3+5, 5+3	8	High risk
5	4+5, 5+4, 5+5	9 and 10	Very high risk

Camelyon16 (Breast Cancer) Dataset. The Camelyon16 dataset is about breast cancer [28]. It is difficult and time-consuming to detect lymph node metastases with gigapixel-sized images. Automated detection of breast cancer metastases in lymph node pictures is of interest. After pre-processing and feature extraction, the resulting dataset has 203 patients, with 80 patients (bags) with cancerous tissue and 123 patients with normal tissue

4.2 Network Architecture

First, we consider a fully connected layer $W_d \in \mathbb{R}^{1024 \times 512}$ with the ReLU activation function to reduce the dimension feature embedding space from 1024 to 512. For the attention network, we consider the gated attention with $U, V \in \mathbb{R}^{256 \times 512}$, each followed by single shared branch $w \in \mathbb{R}^{256 \times 1}$. For the classification network, we choose a fully connected layer $W_c \in \mathbb{R}^{512 \times C}$ where we choose $C = 2$ for binary classification. We use the Adam optimizer [29].

4.3 Tuning Hyper-parameters

To find the best possible model for classification, we consider different hyper-parameters for all methods evaluated in this paper: initial learning rate with values $(10^{-4}, 10^{-3})$, regularization rate $(10^{-5}, 10^{-3})$, and dropout rate $(0.2, 0.5)$. We randomly split data into training/validation/testing datasets (80% training, 10% validation, and 10% training). We train a model on the training dataset for each combination of hyper-parameters until there is no improvement in the validation AUC. We use a stopping criterion [30] with *patience* = 20 epochs (after which there will be no later improvement in AUC on the validation dataset) to determine when to stop training. We use the best model to maximize the validation AUC and report testing AUC.

5   Results

We consider binary classification task and compare four sampling strategies: (1) no sampling where we use whole instances over iterates (this is the standard attention MIL in [13] and what is called CLAM-MIL in [18]), (2) random sampling where we randomly draw choose G instances, (3) adaptive sampling where we adaptively select G instances, and (4) top-k sampling where we choose k instances with the highest attention weights. We evaluate different strategies with both TCGA-PRAD and Camelyon16 datasets. We use the same network architecture, hyper-parameters, and tuning procedure for all methods. For all methods, we choose minimum number of epochs as $e_{min} = 50$, maximum number of epochs as $e_{max} = 300$, and patience $e_{patience} = 20$ for early stopping. For random and adaptive sampling methods, we initially consider ten warm-up epochs ($e_{warm} = 10$) to train the model using whole instances. We conducted all experiments on AWS nodes with one NVIDIA Tesla T4 GPU node, 32 CPUs, and 235 GB of memory. Figure 2 compares the testing AUC, training time, and the number of training epochs (after training is stopped by the early stopping algorithm) for TCGA-PRAD (left panel) and Camelyon16 (right panel). We consider ten repetitions of Monte Carlo simulations for splitting data into training/validation/testing, and we report *mean ± Standard error (SE)*. We observe that all instance sampling strategies reduce the computational complexity as expected. Also, we observe that random instance sampling with enough selected instances (e.g., around $G = 100$ or more) outperforms the no sampling (i.e., using whole instances) strategy. Adaptive sampling might do better than random instance sampling when the number of instances per patient (bag) is minimal (around $G = 10$ or less) due to, e.g., memory constraints. Top-k sampling strategy performs the worst. We discover an important fact: instance sampling strategies (versus using all instances) not only save computing time and resources but also can improve the performance of the patient's disease status with WSI's.

6   Discussion

We investigated different instance sampling strategies for attention-based MIL networks. These strategies significantly reduce computing time (and hence resources). Except for fewer selected instances, random sampling outperforms both the adaptive sampling and no sampling strategies. The justification is that random sampling makes the network sees almost different subsets of instances over different iterates (epochs) and play a role of regularization to avoid overfitting [31].

We used the pre-processing to throw out noisy (e.g., background) tiles or less-informative tiles beforehand. Then we used a pre-trained network (e.g., Resnet50) to extract low dimensional features from remaining image tiles after pre-processing. It is worth investigating more complicated scenarios, e.g., fine-tune some layers of the pre-trained network to extract more distinct and predictive features out of sampled tiles.

We considered a binary classification problem with a small dataset (with 318 patients) to evaluate our proposed model. However, it is worth extending our investigation to multiple-class classification tasks (e.g., the framework presented in [18]) or other tasks such as survival prediction [5, 32, 33].

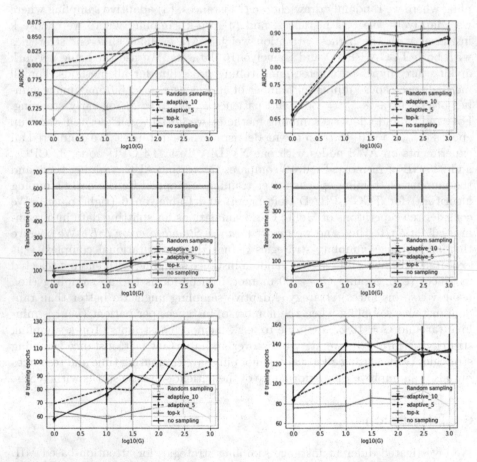

Fig. 2. (left column) TCGA-PRAD (right column) Camelyon16; (top) Area under ROC curve, (middle) training time, and (bottom) number of training epochs; We compare different sampling strategies: **no sampling**, random sampling, **adaptive sampling**, and top-k sampling. (Color figure online)

References

1. Fraggetta, F., Garozzo, S., Zannoni, G.F., Pantanowitz, L., Rossi, E.D.: Routine digital pathology workflow: the Catania experience. J. Pathol. Inform. **8**(51), 1–6 (2017)
2. Epstein, J.I.: An update of the Gleason grading system. J. Urol. **183**(2), 433–440 (2010)
3. Otálora, S., Marini, N., Müller, H., Atzori, M.: Combining weakly and strongly supervised learning improves strong supervision in Gleason pattern classification. BMC Med. Imaging **21**(77), 1–14 (2021)
4. Brunyé, T.T., Mercan, E., Weaver, D.L., Elmore, J.G.: Accuracy is in the eyes of the pathologist: the visual interpretive process and diagnostic accuracy with digital whole slide images. J. Biomed. Info. **66**, 171–179 (2010)
5. Tarkhan, A., Simon, N., Bengtsson, T., Nguyen, K., Dai, J.: Survival prediction using deep learning. In: Proceedings of AAAI Spring Symposium on Survival Prediction - Algorithms, Challenges, and Applications 2021. Proceedings of Machine Learning Research, vol. 146, pp. 207–214. PMLR, 22–24 Mar 2021
6. Cui, M., Zhang, D.Y.: Artificial intelligence and computational pathology. Lab. Invest. **101**, 412–422 (2021)
7. Quellec, G., Cazuguel, G., Cochener, B., Lamard, M.: Multiple-instance learning for medical image and video analysis. IEEE Rev. Biomed. Eng. **10**, 213–234 (2017)
8. Dietterich, T.G., Lathrop, R.H., Lozano-Pérez, T.: Solving the multiple instance problem with axis-parallel rectangles. Artif. Intell. **89**(1), 31–71 (1997)
9. Maron, O., Lozano-Pérez, T.: A framework for multiple-instance learning. In: Jordan, M., Kearns, M., Solla, S. (eds.) Advances in Neural Information Processing Systems, vol. 10. MIT Press (1998)
10. Liu, G., Wu, J., Zhou, Z.-H.: Key instance detection in multi-instance learning. In: Proceedings of the Asian Conference on Machine Learning. Proceedings of Machine Learning Research, vol. 25, pp. 253–268. PMLR (2012)
11. Raffel, C., Ellis, D.P.W.: Feed-forward networks with attention can solve some long-term memory problems (2016)
12. Ramon, J., Raedt, L.D.: Multi instance neural networks. In: ICML Workshop on Attribute-Value and Relational Learning, pp. 53–60 (2000)
13. Ilse, M., Tomczak, J.M., Welling, M.: Attention-based deep multiple instance learning (2018)
14. He, K., Zhang, X., Ren, S., Sun, J.: Deep residual learning for image recognition (2015)
15. Zhu, X., Yao, J., Huang, J.: Deep convolutional neural network for survival analysis with pathological images. In: 2016 IEEE International Conference on Bioinformatics and Biomedicine (BIBM), pp. 544–547 (2016)
16. Wulczyn, E.: Deep learning-based survival prediction for multiple cancer types using histopathology images. PLOS ONE **15**(6), e0233678 (2020)
17. Li, R., Yao, J., Zhu, X., Li, Y., Huang, J.: Graph CNN for survival analysis on whole slide pathological images. In: Frangi, A.F., Schnabel, J.A., Davatzikos, C., Alberola-López, C., Fichtinger, G. (eds.) MICCAI 2018. LNCS, vol. 11071, pp. 174–182. Springer, Cham (2018). https://doi.org/10.1007/978-3-030-00934-2_20
18. Lu, M.Y., Williamson, D.F.K., Chen, T.Y., Chen, R.J., Barbieri, M., Mahmood, F.: Data-efficient and weakly supervised computational pathology on whole-slide images. Nat. Biomed. Eng. **5**, 555–570 (2021)

19. Lu, M.Y., Chen, R.J., Wang, J., Dillon, D., Mahmood, F.: Semi-supervised histology classification using deep multiple instance learning and contrastive predictive coding (2019)
20. Dehaene, O., Camara, A., Moindrot, O., de Lavergne, A., Courtiol, P.: Self-supervision closes the gap between weak and strong supervision in histology (2020)
21. Katharopoulos, A., Fleuret, F.: Processing megapixel images with deep attention-sampling models (2019)
22. Tarkhan, A., Nguyen, T.K., Simon, N., Bengtsson, T., Ocampo, P., Dai, J.: Attention-based deep multiple instance learning with adaptive instance sampling. In: 2022 IEEE 19th International Symposium on Biomedical Imaging (ISBI), pp. 1–5 (2022)
23. Campanella, G., et al.: Clinical-grade computational pathology using weakly supervised deep learning on whole slide images. Nat. Med. **25**, 1–9 (2019)
24. Sharmay, Y., Ehsany, L., Syed, S., Brown, D.E.: HistoTransfer: understanding transfer learning for histopathology. In: 2021 IEEE EMBS International Conference on Biomedical and Health Informatics (BHI), pp. 1–4 (2021)
25. Zuley, M.L., et la.: Radiology data from the cancer genome atlas prostate adenocarcinoma [TCGA-PRAD] collection. Cancer Imaging Arch (2016)
26. Gleason, D.F., Mellinger, G.T.: Prediction of prognosis for prostatic adenocarcinoma by combined histological grading and clinical staging. J. Urol. **111**(1), 58–64 (1974)
27. NCCN: NCCN guidelines: prostate cancer (version 4.2018) (2018). https://www2.tri-kobe.org/nccn/guideline/archive/urological2018/english/prostate.pdf. Accessed 11 Nov 2021
28. Bejnordi, B.E.: Diagnostic assessment of deep learning algorithms for detection of lymph node metastases in women with breast cancer. JAMA **318**(22), 2199–2210 (2017)
29. Kingma, D.P., Ba, J.: Adam: a method for stochastic optimization (2017)
30. Prechelt, L.: Early stopping — but when? In: Montavon, G., Orr, G.B., Müller, K.-R. (eds.) Neural Networks: Tricks of the Trade. LNCS, vol. 7700, pp. 53–67. Springer, Heidelberg (2012). https://doi.org/10.1007/978-3-642-35289-8_5
31. Bishop, C.M.: Training with noise is equivalent to Tikhonov regularization. Neural Comput. **7**(1), 108–116 (1995)
32. Tarkhan, A., Simon, N.: bigSurvSGD: big survival data analysis via stochastic gradient descent. eprint arXiv:2003.00116 [math, stat] (2020)
33. Yao, J., Zhu, X., Jonnagaddala, J., Hawkins, N., Huang, J.: Whole slide images based cancer survival prediction using attention guided deep multiple instance learning networks. Med. Image Anal. **65**, 101789 (2020)

Masked Video Modeling with Correlation-Aware Contrastive Learning for Breast Cancer Diagnosis in Ultrasound

Zehui Lin[1,2,3], Ruobing Huang[1,2,3]([✉]), Dong Ni[1,2,3], Jiayi Wu[4], and Baoming Luo[4]

[1] National-Regional Key Technology Engineering Laboratory for Medical Ultrasound, School of Biomedical Engineering, Health Science Center, Shenzhen University, Shenzhen, China
ruobing.huang@szu.edu.cn
[2] Medical Ultrasound Image Computing (MUSIC) Lab, Shenzhen University, Shenzhen, China
[3] Marshall Laboratory of Biomedical Engineering, Shenzhen University, Shenzhen, China
[4] Department of Ultrasound, Sun Yat-Sen Memorial Hospital of Sun Yat-Sen University, Guangzhou, China

Abstract. Breast cancer is one of the leading causes of cancer deaths in women. As the primary output of breast screening, breast ultrasound (US) video contains exclusive dynamic information for cancer diagnosis. However, training models for video analysis is non-trivial as it requires a voluminous dataset which is also expensive to annotate. Furthermore, the diagnosis of breast lesion faces unique challenges such as inter-class similarity and intra-class variation. In this paper, we propose a pioneering approach that directly utilizes US videos in computer-aided breast cancer diagnosis. It leverages masked video modeling as pretraning to reduce reliance on dataset size and detailed annotations. Moreover, a correlation-aware contrastive loss is developed to facilitate the identifying of the internal and external relationship between benign and malignant lesions. Experimental results show that our proposed approach achieved promising classification performance and can outperform other state-of-the-art methods.

1 Introduction

Being painless, cost-effective and radiation-free, ultrasound (US) imaging is widely used in breast cancer screening [2], especially for the evaluation of dense breasts [11]. Its real-time imaging capability allows rapid acquisition of tissue information and produces corresponding US image sequences (i.e., videos) on the screen instantaneously. Compared with the single conventional 2D static image, the original US video of a lesion contains richer spatial-temporal information

X. Xu et al. (Eds.): REMIA 2022, LNCS 13543, pp. 105–114, 2022.
https://doi.org/10.1007/978-3-031-16876-5_11

and is beneficial for diagnosis [14,15]. However, deciphering raw US videos faces several challenges, including heavy data-oriented dependency, scarce supervision signals, inter-class similarity and intra-class variance (see Fig. 1). A tailored computer-aided diagnostic (CAD) tool is needed to address these challenges and better assist clinicians to prevent misdiagnosis and overtreatment.

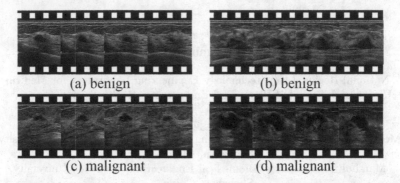

(a) benign   (b) benign

(c) malignant   (d) malignant

Fig. 1. Breast ultrasound video examples. (a), (b) indicate benign cases and (c), (d) indicate malignant ones. A video contains hundreds of frames, each of which comprises a full 2D US image. Each video has a binary label (i.e. benign or malignant)–extreme sparse supervision signals compare to the data size. Besides, the lesions have a diverse appearance and complex surrounding tissues that brings additional challenges to the classification.

A considerable amount of 2D static image works have been proposed to help sonographers in diagnosing breast cancer [3]. Traditional methods typically extract handcraft textural features. For example, Flores et al. [7] analyzed morphological and texture features and used a features selection methodology to improve the classification performance of breast tumors on ultrasonography. Recently, deep learning models are favoured in designing new CAD tools due to their strong representation learning ability. For example, Zeimarani et al. [16] used a custom-built convolutional neural network (CNN) with a few hidden layers and applied regularization techniques to improve the diagnostic performance using 2D US. These 2D approaches have demonstrated promising results while they are unable to handle video data with excessive dimension and scarce labels. Some researchers have investigated ways to directly utilize US videos of other organs or other modalities. In [5], Chen et al. exploited contrastive learning to initialize video model for US videos of lung and liver. Another group focused on contrast-enhanced US [4] and proposed to add additional attention modules on a 3D CNN backbone to classify lesions. These methods have their own merits while they neglect the natural spatiotemporal patterns that lie within the video.

In this paper, we propose a novel video classification framework, named Masked Video modeling with Correlation-aware Contrastive learning (MVCC), to address the challenges in breast cancer diagnosis. Our contribution is threefold. First, to the best of our knowledge, this is the first study that directly utilizes the videos of common B-mode Breast US for breast nodule identification. Second, we proposed to use masked video modeling to fully exploit limited data and exiguous annotations. Different from the 2D approach [8], a dual-level masking strategy is adopted to explicitly extract features in both the spatial and temporal dimensions. Third, we selectively constrain the high-level representations to combat intra-class variation and inter-class similarity through a novel correlation-aware contrastive loss. Validation experiments showed that the proposed method was able to process rich video information and identify the breast nodules accurately.

2 Methodology

To fully exploit the limited annotation and available data, we propose to equip the classification model with masked video modeling and correlation-aware contrastive learning. Figure 2 displays the overall framework. A TimeSfomer-based [1] auto-encoder is first built and pre-trained with a novel dual-level masking strategy to fully capture the spatial and temporal dependencies in a self-supervised manner. The weight of the trained encoder is then retained and fine-tuned using the ground truth labels. Furthermore, the model is constrained by a correlation-aware contrastive loss to selectively encourage feature resemblance among the same class, while explicitly penalizing this among different classes. Details are explained in the following section.

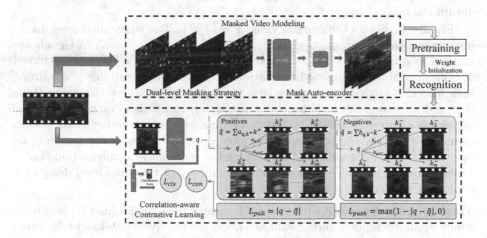

Fig. 2. Overview of our proposed framework.

2.1 Masked Video Modeling

In video analysis, state-of-the-art deep learning models with growing capacity and capability can easily overfit, even on large datasets. Meanwhile, annotating video dataset is extremely time- and labour-demanding. As a result, training deep learning based video analysis model is non-trivial. On the other hand, videos naturally contain rich spatial-temporal context information, reflecting the structures of normal tissues and lesions. To exploit this, we leverage self-supervised learning to prepare the model for the downstream video classification task. In specific, we opt for an auto-encoder approach that reconstructs the original video given its partial observation. In other words, a video x is masked based on strategy $S : x \rightarrow \hat{x}$. $\hat{x}$ is then passed to an auto-encoder $De(En(\hat{x}))$ to reconstruct the original video from the masked data by minimizing the difference between its output $\bar{x}$ and x, s.t. $\bar{x} = De(En(\hat{x}))$. $En()$ represents the encoder part while $De()$ represents the decoder. This pre-training task helps to learn informative low-level patterns and understand the global context contains in videos, consequently, could provide a good initialization for the subsequent downstream task.

Dual-Level Masking Strategy. Some studies have investigated image-based masking strategies, while extending this technique to video faces the additional temporal dimension and more severe information redundancy. To explicitly extract information from both spatial and temporal dimensions, we propose a dual-level masking strategy. In particular, define an input video $x = \{f_a\}_1^t, a = 1, 2, ...t$. The t frames of x is randomly selected and masked, producing $x' = \{f_{a'}\}_1^{t'}, t' < t$. The frame-level masking ratio is controlled by α, which satisfies $t' = t \times \alpha$. Next, each frame $f_{a'}$ in x' are divided into regular non-overlapping patches for patch-level masking. $\beta\%$ of patches are removed and obtain the masked frame $f'_{a'}$.

Finally, we obtain the masked video $\hat{x} = \{f'_{a'}\}_1^{t'}$. The whole dual-level masking strategy can be summarized as $S : x \rightarrow x' \rightarrow \hat{x}$, and $\alpha+(1-\alpha)\beta\%$ signals are masked in total. This dual-level masking strategy explicitly forces the removal of both spatial and temporal information, creating a more suitable pre-training task for video analysis. As can be seen in Fig. 2, the patch-level masking (blue dots and arrows) erases local patches and requires comprehension over the tissue appearance for restoration. The frame-level masking, on the other hand, breaks connectivity in the temporal space (orange dots and arrows) and can only be recovered based on understanding over global anatomical configuration. Later experimental results also demonstrate the efficacy of this dual-level design for exploiting video data.

Masked Auto-Encoder. Our encoder leverages the TimeSformer [1] backbone which applies temporal and spatial attention separately in sub-blocks. Inspired by [8], we design a decoder using a lightweight transformer structure [8] and is only used during the pre-training phase. The input of the MAE decoder is the full set of tokens consisting of (i) encoded visible signal, and (ii) masked tokens. Positional embeddings [6] are added to all tokens to provide location information. The decoder reconstructs the input pixel values for each masked token and we use mean squared error (MSE) loss to compute the difference between $\hat{x}$ and x in the pixel space (only on masked patches). The asymmetric design over encoder and decoder creates an opportunity for saving computation and training time.

2.2 Correlation-Aware Contrastive Learning

The core of contrastive learning is to learn the representations which maximize the agreement between the similar, related instances (i.e., positives) and minimize the similarity between the different and unrelated instances (i.e., negatives) at the same time. Supervised contrastive learning [10] leverages the label information to construct the positive and negative samples and have shown promising results on many applications. However, it overlooks the fact that samples from the same class could have a dramatically different appearance (see Fig. 1 (c) and (d)). Imposing similarity constraints to these samples might confuse the model and jeopardize convergence. Furthermore, the most challenging examples to classify are those who share similar features while belonging to different classes (see Fig. 1 (a) and (c)). Therefore, we propose to take the correlation among samples into account in contrastive learning. In other words, correlated, ambiguous negative samples are heavily penalized to maximize the margin between decision surface. Meanwhile, the impact of uncorrelated positive samples is de-emphasized to allow flexible representation.

Formally, a query video x is passed to the encoder to produce high-level representation $q = En(x)$. Within a training batch, the representation of positive samples (sharing same label with the query) can be denoted as $k_i^+ \in P = \{k_1^+, k_2^+, \cdots, k_m^+\}$ and the negative samples (sharing different labels with the query) is denoted as $k_i^- \in N = \{k_1^-, k_2^-, \cdots, k_n^-\}$. The positively-correlated representation $\hat{q}$ is calculated as:

$$\hat{q} = \sum_{k_i^+ \in P} a_{q,k_i^+} k_i^+, \qquad (1)$$

where a_{q,k_i^+} is the normalized similarity of q and k_i^+, which is defined as:

$$a_{q,k_i^+} = \frac{exp\left(sim\left(q, k_i^+\right)/\tau\right)}{\sum_{k' \in P} exp\left(sim\left(q, k'\right)/\tau\right)}, \qquad (2)$$

where τ is the temperature and $sim(y,z) = y^T z/\|y\|\|z\|$ measures the cosine similarity. The negatively-correlated representation $\check{q}$ is calculated in the same manner as:

$$\check{q} = \sum_{k_i^- \in N} b_{q,k_i^-} k_i^-, \qquad (3)$$

where b_{q,k_i^-} is defined as:

$$b_{q,k_i^-} = \frac{exp\left(sim\left(q, k_i^-\right)/\tau\right)}{\sum_{k' \in N} exp\left(sim\left(q, k'\right)/\tau\right)}. \qquad (4)$$

The core of this procedure is to reconstruct the query sample based on its proximity with each positive (or negative) sample in high-level semantics. This design can highlight similar negative samples while understating the dis-similar positive ones, producing smoothed and correlation-sensible representations to calculate the contrastive loss. To combat the varying issues in differentiating the query sample against different classes, we compose the loss function with two elements. The positive element utilizes $\hat{q}$, and can be defined as:

$$L_{pull} = |q - \hat{q}|. \tag{5}$$

Similarly, the negative element can be defined as:

$$L_{push} = max\left(1 - |q - \check{q}|, 0\right), \tag{6}$$

forming the full correlation-aware contrastive loss as:

$$L_{con} = L_{pull} + L_{push}. \tag{7}$$

$|\cdot|$ represents L_1 loss. $max\left(\cdot, 0\right)$ indicates the Hinge loss [12] which is able to maintain equilibrium in the optimization. L_{con}, therefore, neglects dis-similar positive samples to and only pulls together the similar one. Meanwhile, it deliberately pushes away similar negative samples while neglecting the distant ones which can be easily classified. In this way, the model allows distinct positive samples to have different features to handle intra-class variation, while mining hard negative examples to combat inter-class similarity. The overall objective is a combination of the standard cross-entropy loss L_{cls} and the correlation-aware contrastive loss L_{con}, defined as:

$$L = L_{cls} + \lambda L_{con}, \tag{8}$$

where λ is a balancing factor of the two learning targets.

3   Experiments and Results

Dataset and Implementation Details. The in-house dataset contains 3854 breast ultrasound videos (with size 224×224, average 260 frames) approved by the local IRB. The videos were collected by different operators using different US machines. Each video contains one lesion of a patient, while its corresponding ground truth is derived from the biopsy result. Overall, the benign-to-malignant ratio is approximately 3 to 1. The dataset was randomly split into 2697, 385 and 772 videos for training, validation and independent testing. All experiments were repeated for 4 times with different random seeds and the averaged performance was reported to produce statistically stable results. The value of λ in Eq. 8 was empirically set to 0.1. We use the SGD optimizer with a learning rate of 0.0075. Different augmentation strategies were applied, including scaling, flipping, and cropping. We implemented our method in *Pytorch*, using an NVIDIA RTX 3090 GPU. In this study, model performance is evaluated using accuracy (ACC (%)), sensitivity (SEN (%)), specificity (SPE (%)), precision (PRE (%)) and F1-score (%).

Quantitative Analysis. We first investigate whether and how the performance of the classification model changes with or without different contrastive learning strategy (conducted without using masked video modeling). We select the state-of-the-art video recognition model–TimeSformer [1] as a strong baseline (trained only using cross-entropy). We then apply the classical supervised contrastive loss [10] (denoted as '+SCL') and the proposed correlation-aware contrastive loss (denoted as '+C-SCL').

Experimental results are reported in row 1–3 Table 1. The TimeSformer baseline alone obtained good accuracy (89.15%), while the sensitivity is relatively low (73.84%). This may result from fewer true positive predictions. The SCL helped to further increase the accuracy and specificity (row 2, Table 1), which may result from its ability to constraint representations in the embedding space. However, its sensitivity score is even lower (73.54%), indicating a strong bias to the dominant negative class. On the other hand, the proposed C-SCL increases the sensitivity by 3.02%, which is critical for identifying malignant nodules. This may stem from that the C-SCL explicitly pull away representations of malignant cases from similar benign ones. Furthermore, it avoids penalizing dissimilar features from the same class and may help to alleviate over-fitting. As a result, the Baseline+C-SCL combination produced the highest F1-score (80.59%). Also, note that the design of the C-SCL is general and does not require alteration of the model architecture. It could be easily extended to other image analysis tasks without bell and whistle.

Table 1. The mean (std) results of different methods on the breast video classification.

Method	ACC (%)	SEN (%)	SPE (%)	PRE (%)	F1-score (%)
Baseline	89.15(0.65)	73.84(1.34)	94.71(1.25)	83.68(3.09)	78.38(1.11)
+SCL [10]	89.99(1.30)	73.54(5.23)	95.94(0.34)	86.75(1.20)	79.52(3.55)
+C-SCL	90.28(1.06)	76.56(6.32)	95.23(0.83)	85.46(1.29)	80.59(3.32)
USCL [5]	83.72(1.08)	51.27(6.25)	94.52(1.53)	76.12(3.82)	60.98(4.71)
CVRL [13]	79.21(0.19)	43.89(10.99)	92.07(3.89)	68.38(5.64)	52.14(5.80)
MVCC-Patch	90.42(1.50)	74.16(3.84)	96.30(0.98)	87.85(3.36)	80.41(3.50)
MVCC-Frame	90.28(0.95)	75.54(1.90)	95.64(1.19)	86.34(3.54)	80.54(1.97)
MVCC	90.64(1.10)	76.02(1.83)	95.95(1.07)	87.21(3.27)	81.21(2.27)

Next, we discuss whether masked video modeling can provide a better initialization and the influence of different masking strategies. In specific, two state-of-the-art (SOTA) video pretraining methods: USCL [5] and CVRL [13] are compared with our method. We use the patch-level only, frame-level only and the proposed dual-level masking strategy respectively to pre-train the classification model. Note that the patch-level strategy is essentially similar to [8], which was proposed to analyse 2D images.

Table 1 shows the results (row 4–8). As we can see that the SOTA methods gain low sensitivity and F1-score (row 4–5). We conjecture this may be due to some hard examples sharing similar features while belonging to different classes failing these methods, resulting in poor initialization and local optimum. Compared with natural video dataset k400 [9] initialization (row 3) the patch-level masking approach obtained higher accuracy, specificity and precision, proves itself as a useful initialization technique to the normal natural data pretraining. It is interesting to see the frame-level masking strategy alone does not lead to performance gain (compare row 7 to row 3). This may result from that there exists information redundancy and the frame-level masking cannot assist the extraction of anatomical features than lies within the spatial dimension. On the contrary, the proposed dual-level masking strategy utilizes both spatial and temporal information and scored the highest accuracy (90.64%) and F1-score (81.21%) among all competing methods. It is worth noting that despite facing an imbalanced dataset (fewer malignant samples), our approach were still able to gain high sensitivity, and ultimately the overall performance.

Qualitative Analysis. We further employed T-SNE and Gradient-weighted Class Activation Mapping (Grad-CAM) to visualize the representation distribution and model decisions. As shown in Fig. 3, we mainly compared baseline, C-SCL and our complete framework. For the representation distribution, (b) and (c) is clearly better than (a) that the samples are more aggregated. Our method can make it easier for classifiers to construct decision boundaries. It can be observed from Grad-CAM visualization that the interpretability of high attention regions is poor on the baseline while the C-SCL model only focused on

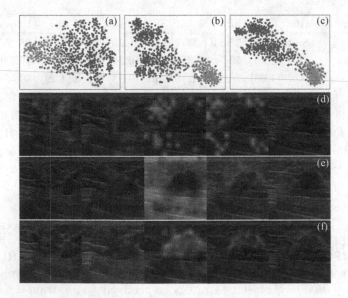

Fig. 3. T-SNE and Grad-CAM visualization. (a) and (d) correspond to the baseline. (b) and (e) correspond to the correlation-aware contrastive learning without masked video modeling (i.e. C-SCL). (c) and (f) correspond to MVCC(+C-SCL).

the area around the nodule. Our model precisely focused on the nodule regions during classification despite no location information being given.

4 Conclusions

In this paper, we proposed the first research about breast ultrasound video diagnosis for breast cancer. Thanks to masked video modeling and correlation-aware contrastive learning, the proposed learning framework can efficiently solve the challenge of video recognition under scarce supervised signals and complex nodule patterns. Experiments on a large-scale breast ultrasound video dataset prove the efficacy and flexibility of the proposed framework. Future research will focus on extending this framework to ultrasound videos of other organs and videos of other modalities.

References

1. Bertasius, G., Wang, H., Torresani, L.: Is space-time attention all you need for video understanding? arXiv preprint arXiv:2102.05095 (2021)
2. Brem, R.F., Lenihan, M.J., Lieberman, J., Torrente, J.: Screening breast ultrasound: past, present, and future. Am. J. Roentgenol. **204**(2), 234–240 (2015)
3. Chan, H.P., Samala, R.K., Hadjiiski, L.M.: CAD and AI for breast cancer-recent development and challenges. Br. J. Radiol. **93**(1108), 20190580 (2019)
4. Chen, C., Wang, Y., Niu, J., Liu, X., Li, Q., Gong, X.: Domain knowledge powered deep learning for breast cancer diagnosis based on contrast-enhanced ultrasound videos. IEEE Trans. Med. Imaging **40**, 2439–2451 (2021)
5. Chen, Y., et al.: USCL: pretraining deep ultrasound image diagnosis model through video contrastive representation learning. In: de Bruijne, M., et al. (eds.) MICCAI 2021. LNCS, vol. 12908, pp. 627–637. Springer, Cham (2021). https://doi.org/10.1007/978-3-030-87237-3_60
6. Dosovitskiy, A., et al.: An image is worth 16×16 words: transformers for image recognition at scale. arXiv preprint arXiv:2010.11929 (2020)
7. Flores, W.G., de Albuquerque Pereira, W.C., Infantosi, A.F.C.: Improving classification performance of breast lesions on ultrasonography. Pattern Recogn. **48**(4), 1125–1136 (2015)
8. He, K., Chen, X., Xie, S., Li, Y., Dollár, P., Girshick, R.: Masked autoencoders are scalable vision learners. arXiv preprint arXiv:2111.06377 (2021)
9. Kay, W., et al.: The kinetics human action video dataset. arXiv preprint arXiv:1705.06950 (2017)
10. Khosla, P., et al.: Supervised contrastive learning. arXiv preprint arXiv:2004.11362 (2020)
11. Nothacker, M., et al.: Early detection of breast cancer: benefits and risks of supplemental breast ultrasound in asymptomatic women with mammographically dense breast tissue. a systematic review. BMC Cancer **9**(1), 1–9 (2009)
12. Platt, J.: Sequential minimal optimization: a fast algorithm for training support vector machines (1998)
13. Qian, R., et al.: Spatiotemporal contrastive video representation learning. In: Proceedings of the IEEE/CVF Conference on Computer Vision and Pattern Recognition, pp. 6964–6974 (2021)

14. Yang, D., et al.: Section discrepancy and diagnostic performance of breast lesions in two-dimensional ultrasound by dynamic videos versus static images. BIO Integr. **3**, 61–70 (2021)
15. Youk, J.H., et al.: Comparison of inter-observer variability and diagnostic performance of the fifth edition of BI-RADS for breast ultrasound of static versus video images. Ultrasound Med. Biol. **42**(9), 2083–2088 (2016)
16. Zeimarani, B., Costa, M.G.F., Nurani, N.Z., Bianco, S.R., Pereira, W.C.D.A., Costa Filho, C.F.F.: Breast lesion classification in ultrasound images using deep convolutional neural network. IEEE Access **8**, 133349–133359 (2020)

A Self-attentive Meta-learning Approach for Image-Based Few-Shot Disease Detection

Achraf Ouahab, Olfa Ben-Ahmed$^{(\boxtimes)}$, and Christine Fernandez-Maloigne

XLIM Research Institute, URM CNRS 7252, University of Poitiers, Poitiers, France
olfa.ben.ahmed@univ-poitiers.fr

Abstract. In this paper, we propose a few-shot medical images classification framework for low prevalence disease detection. The proposed method leans to transfer medical knowledge from common diseases to low prevalence cases using meta-learning. Indeed, compared to natural images, medical images vary less diversely from one image to another, with complex patterns and less semantic information. Hence, extracting clinically relevant features and learning a disease-specific signature from few images is challenging. Inspired by clinician's cognitive and visual diagnosis, we integrate an attention mechanism in the meta-learning process and we revised the meta-loss function to learn clinically disease-specific features over tasks. The proposed approach has been evaluated on two image-based diagnosis problems namely low prevalence skin and low prevalence thorax diseases diagnosis. We obtained respectively for those two use-cases 84.3% and 73.4% of average AUC in 2-way 5-shot classification setting. Obtained results demonstrate the effectiveness of the proposed framework compared to baselines and state-of the-art few-shot disease detection methods.

Keywords: Few-Shot Learning · Meta-learning · Visual attention · Rare/Low prevalence disease diagnosis

1 Introduction

Nowadays, Deep Learning (DL) techniques have achieved a breakthrough in the field of Artificial Intelligence. Especially, DL-based approaches have seen an impressively good performance in image analysis domain. However, huge, labeled data-sets are needed to train on. Collecting such extensive annotated images is time and resources consuming and it is not feasible for real-world applications, especially in the medical domain [1]. Indeed, unlike the case of natural images, where annotations can be easily performed by non-experts, medical images annotation requires careful and time-consuming analysis from experts such as radiologists. Furthermore, annotated images for rare or novel diseases are likely to remain scarce due the very low prevalence of certain diseases in population and the limited clinical expertise to annotate such data [2]. The limited availability

© The Author(s), under exclusive license to Springer Nature Switzerland AG 2022
X. Xu et al. (Eds.): REMIA 2022, LNCS 13543, pp. 115–125, 2022.
https://doi.org/10.1007/978-3-031-16876-5_12

of annotated medical imaging data remains the biggest challenge for the success of DL techniques in real world clinical scenarios.

In medicine, radiology trainers are often required to transfer knowledge from what they have learned previously to perform few-shot diagnosis in their experiential training progression [3]. Yet, radiologists are trained over several years and gained experience from similar seen diagnosis tasks to understand the clinical relevance of features and resolve a new task. In practice, experienced radiologist diagnoses new unseen disease by using prior-knowledge acquired from related tasks (common diseases) and generalizes to new tasks. Moreover, radiologists visually focus their attention on some regions of interest and learn clinically relevant visual features while disregarding unnecessary features to make diagnosis [4].

In this paper, we propose a self-attentive meta-learning approach for few-shot disease detection. Inspired by radiologist image-based visual diagnosis, we design an attention mechanism to learn clinically visual relevant features across tasks. Indeed, the attention mechanism guides the few-shot learner to focus on clinically relevant features of the image for each task and hence refines the task features representation for better knowledge transfer. By this way, the model is learning to learn class discrimination through learning where to pay attention from one task to another in the same way as a radiologist. We believe that such learning strategy would draw a more refined and discriminating feature space by focusing on relevant and salient features in a task while implicitly learns to suppress irrelevant features (background, noise, non related-disease features, etc.). The remainder of this paper is organized as follows. In Sect. 2, we discuss existing works on few-shot medical image analysis. Section 3 presents the proposed approach. In Sect. 4, experimental results and comparison with State-Of-The-Art (SOTA) methods are carried out. Finally, Sect. 5 concludes the work and opens some research perspectives.

2 Related Work

Few-Shot Learning (FSL), a new paradigm that learns a prediction model from small amount of labeled data, has been recently attract much attention [5]. In general, FSL methods learn a model that can quickly generalize to new tasks from few labeled samples [8]. A special progress in FSL for computer vision field has been made using the so-called meta-learning paradigm [6]. Meta learning is inspired from the way that human thinks and learns. This paradigm, also known as "learn to learn", provides an opportunity to tackle conventional challenges of DL, including data bottleneck and model generalization. Indeed, meta-learning consists in learning new skills from similar few-shot tasks to learn how to adapt a model to a new task for which only a few labeled samples are available [7].

Meta-learning approaches have seen great success in FSL of natural images [6]. Recently, meta-learning has been investigated for medical images segmentation [11–13] achieving promising performances. However, methods that address the problem of few-shot medical image diagnosis remain very scarce. Small body of works have been recently proposed for few-shot medical image classification with the aim of disease diagnosis. For instance, Yuan et al. proposed a fast adaptation and an active meta-learning framework for brain cell classification [14]. Maicas et al. proposed curriculum learning based FSL method for breast screening from Magnitude Resonance Imaging (MRI). In order to solve the problem of long-tailed distributions of annotated images for dermathological diseases detection, Gabriel et al. [15] improved the Model Agnostic Meta-Learning (MAML) algorithm [16] by adding a teacher-student curriculum learning as a new way to select tasks. Mahajan et al. [28] proposed methods that use Reptile [17] and Prototypical networks [18] for the same diagnosis task. In the later work, the authors incorporated Group Equivariant convolutions (G-convolutions) to facilitate quick adaptation of deep neural networks. In the same context, Li et al. [19] proposed a difficulty-aware meta-learning method that monitors the importance of learning tasks during meta-training while Prabhu et al. [20] modeled the intra-class variability using Prototypical Clustering Networks for few-shot learning. Yet, Rishav et al. [21] proposed a gradient-based meta-learning approach for medical image classification. They proposed to regularize their model using different augmentation techniques. Recently, some works have been proposed for COVID-19 detection using meta-learning [22–24].

Meta-learning could be a potential solution to overcome the limitation of DL traditional approaches in the medical domain by learning from only few small medical imaging data for disease diagnosis. However, traditional approaches did not leverage clinically relevant features similar to trained radiologists and just learn generic features over tasks. Hence, they failed to learn a strong diagnosis-specific representation from only few images over tasks. Indeed, considering the specificity of medical images (noise, irrelevant background information, non clinically relevant features, small inter-class variability, etc.), a general high-dimensional features representation may not be enough to discriminate between diseases. Recently, Paul et al. [25] proposed a saliency-based model to classify Chest X-Ray images in an FSL framework. However, in [25], salient features extraction and classification were performed in two independent phases. An end-to-end training for salient image information along with classification would be more efficient for learning and transferring disease-specific knowledge from few images.

3   Proposed Approach

We formulate the low prevalence/rare diseases diagnosis task as a few-shot classification problem (N-way k-shot) [7]. Here, we aim to discriminate between N classes with k examples of each class (k very small). The proposed meta-learning based diagnosis consists of two stages: meta-training and meta-testing. In the meta-training stage, a model is learned in an episodic fashion across a set of common previously seen tasks (e.g., common diseases). Then, in the meta-testing stage, the learned model (base-learner) is used to resolve the new few samples task (e.g., rare disease). We note $D_{meta-train}$ and $D_{meta-test}$ the images datasets used to sample tasks for respectively the meta-train and the meta-test phases. Every task is composed of a Support set (S) of $N \times k$ samples to adjust the model parameters to the specific task, and a Query set (Q) of N samples to evaluate the base-learner.

Self-attention Base-Learner. Figure 1 presents the proposed self-attention base-learner model, composed of 3 blocks: feature extraction block, classification block and self-Attention branch.

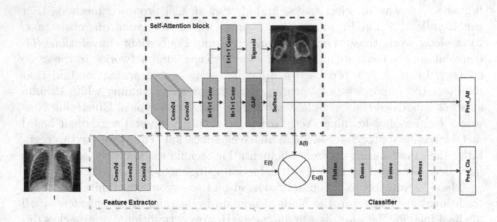

Fig. 1. Self-attention base-learner architecture

The feature extraction branch is a 3 convolution blocks. Each one consists of (3×3) convolution layer with 32 filters, followed by a ReLU function. We use batch normalization in order to reduce model over-fitting. For an input image I, this branch outputs a feature map $E(I)$. This feature map is fed to the attention branch for refinement using the attention mechanism.

The attention branch produces an attention map that explicitly indicates the location in the image that the model relies on to make predictions ($Pred\_Att$). It is composed of convolution blocks to extract task-specific features. The feature map is then fed to two other blocks, the first consists of a $N \times 1 \times 1$ Convolution block to extract the heat map corresponding to each class of N classes, a $1 \times 1 \times 1$ Convolution block followed and normalized by a Sigmoid function to produce the global attention map that will be used along side with the output of the feature extractor as inputs for the attention mechanism. The latter block consists of two $N \times 1 \times 1$ convolution blocks, a Global Average Pooling (GAP) layer and a Softmax layer to output the attention block predictions ($Pred\_Att$).

$A(I)$ is the output attention map produced by the self-attention block for an input image I. The attention mechanism refines the features maps by keeping only clinically relevant information and filer-out noise and non-relevant features for the task. It produces the refined feature map $E_A(I) = E(I) * A(I)$. Then, $E_A(I)$ is fed to the classification branch for output prediction. The classifier branch is composed of a flatten layer, two dense layers of respectively 512 and N neurons, and a softmax function for predictions ($Pred\_Cla$).

Meta-training Phase (Learning from Common Diseases). Let f be the base-learner model parameterized by θ randomly initialized weights, and $p(T)$ is the tasks distribution from the meta-training data-set. In the meta-training phase, we aim to find the optimal initialization of θ from the distribution of similar related tasks. Indeed, the meta-learner intends to optimize the weights θ at each iteration by using prior knowledge and by learning where to pay attention from one task to another. Here, a clinically relevant task-specific representation is learned such that a simple fine-tune of the base-learner in the new task with few gradient-descent steps is enough for the model to perform well in meta-testing phase. The meta-training process is described in Algorithm 1. The inner loop aims to adapt the initial parameters θ of the model f_θ to a specific task T_i. In Algorithm 1, parameters are updated using a gradient descent step with a learning rate α. During this inner-update step the sum of attention branch and classification branch losses (Eq. 1) is minimized.

Algorithm 1. Meta-training: Learning from common diseases

Require: $p(T)$: distribution over tasks $\in D_{meta-train}$
Require: α & β Learning and meta-learning learning rates
1: randomly initialize θ
2: **while** number of meta-epochs is not done **do** //*outer loop*
3:     Sample batch of tasks $T_i \sim p(T) \in D_{meta-train}$
4:     **for all** T_i **do** //*inner loop*
5:         Sample K data samples $D_i^S = \{x_j, y_j\}$ from T_i
6:         Evaluate $\nabla_\theta \mathcal{L}_{T_i}(f_\theta, D_i^S)$ using $\mathcal{L}_{T_i}$ in eq (1)
7:         Compute adapted parameters with gradient descent:
            $\theta_i' \leftarrow \theta - \alpha \nabla_\theta \mathcal{L}_{T_i}(f_\theta, D_i^S)$
8:         Sample data samples $D_i^Q = \{x_j, y_j\}$ from T_i for
            the meta-update
9:     **end for**
10:    Compute $\mathcal{L}_T(f_\theta)_{\{Cla\}}$ Eq. (3) and $\mathcal{L}_T(f_\theta)_{\{Att\}}$ Eq. (4) on batch
11:    Update the model parameters θ using the Eq. (5)
12 **end while**

Both losses are calculated using the binary cross-entropy loss (Eq. 2).

$$\mathcal{L}_{T_i}(f_\theta, D_i^S) = \mathcal{L}_{T_i}(f_\theta, D_i^S)_{\{Att\}} + \mathcal{L}_{T_i}(f_\theta, D_i^S)_{\{Cla\}} \qquad (1)$$

$$\mathcal{L}(f_\theta, D) = - \sum_{(x_j, y_j) \sim D} y_j log(f_\theta(x_j)) + (1 - y_j) log(1 - f_\theta(x_j)) \qquad (2)$$

where x_j is the input sample, and y_j stands for the ground truth label.

For each task T_i, after few steps of training the model f_θ on the support set D_i^S, we get the optimal parameters θ_i' that fits the best the task T_i.

In the meta optimization phase (outer loop), a meta-update is performed on the initial optimization parameters to move it to a better initial position.

We update the parameters using the gradients of the sum of classification losses $\mathcal{L}_T(f_\theta)_{\{Cla\}}$ (Eq. 3) over tasks of the same batch, and we used the attention loss as a factor in the meta-update learning rate to penalize the meta-update when high attention losses are encountered (Eq. 5).

$$\mathcal{L}_T(f_\theta)_{\{Cla\}} = \sum_{T_i \sim p(T)} \mathcal{L}(f_{\theta'_i}, D_i^Q)_{\{Cla\}} \qquad (3)$$

$$\mathcal{L}_T(f_\theta)_{\{Att\}} = \sum_{T_i \sim p(T)} \mathcal{L}(f_{\theta'_i}, D_i^Q)_{\{Att\}} \qquad (4)$$

$$\theta \leftarrow \theta - \beta(1 - \tanh(\mathcal{L}_T(f_\theta)_{\{Att\}}))\nabla_\theta \mathcal{L}_T(f_\theta)_{\{Cla\}} \qquad (5)$$

where θ are the initial base-learner parameters, β is the meta-update hyper-parameter, $\mathcal{L}_T(f_\theta)_{\{Att\}}$ is the sum of attention losses over the tasks of a sampled batch of tasks, $\nabla_\theta \mathcal{L}_T(f_\theta)_{\{Cla\}}$ is the gradient of the classification loss resulted over the tasks of a sampled batch of tasks T with respect to θ.

Meta-testing Phase (Low prevalence/rare Diseases detection). We formulate tasks-related episodes (D_i^S, D_i^Q) from never-seen classes during training represented by rare diseases. For a given testing task T_i from $D_{meta-test}$, we respect the same N-way k-shot settings as the one used during training. The knowledge learned (Weights) in the meta-training phase is used to initialize the final classifier instead of traditional random initialization.

4   Experiments and Results

4.1   Experimental Settings

In order to evaluate the performance of the proposed approach, we simulate two medical diagnosis problems: Low prevalence/rare skin diseases detection from dermoscopic images and low prevalence thorax diseases detection from Chest X-Ray data through two public imaging datasets. First, we use skin lesion images from 7 skin diseases from the ISIC 2018 [26] dataset, including Melanocytic Nevus (NV) (6705), Melanoma (MEL) (1113), benign Keratosis (BKL) (1099), Basal Cell Carcinoma (BCC)(514), Actinic Keratosis (AKIEC)(327), Vascular Lesion (VASC)(142) and Dermatofibroma (DF)(115). Second, we use the public Chest X-Ray NHI 14 dataset [27] to simulate the problem of few-shot classification for low prevalence thorax diseases detection problem from Chest X-Ray data. This data-set contains $112,120$ frontal-view X-Ray images of $30,805$ unique patients with a labeled 14 thoracic pathologist images. In this paper, we will focus on single label classification and hence we select only images labeled with only a single disease class. We retain Chest X-Ray images for 14 diseases including Atelectasis (2210), Consolidation (346), Infiltration (5270), Pneumothorax (1506), Edema (51), Emphysema (525), Fibrosis (648), Effusion (2086), Pneumonia (176), Pleural-thickening (875), Cardiomegaly (746), Nodule (1924), Mass (1367) and Hernia (98). A 15th class is added in meta-train: if an X-Ray

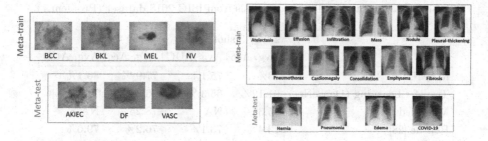

Fig. 2. Meta-train (blue) and meta-test (orange) partition

image contains no abnormalities, it is labeled as "No Finding" (4500). We added 120 chest X-Ray images of COVID-19 infected patients from [29]. We simulate the low prevalence disease detection problem by using the classes with largest amount of cases as common diseases (i.e., meta-train data) and the left classes as the low prevalence diseases (i.e., meta-test data). Figure 2 illustrates images samples for the meta-train and meta-test data-sets. For both few diagnosis problems, we created binary classification tasks for meta-training and meta-testing stages.

- **Meta-training**: we query k images from the $D_{meta-train}$ for each of the two classes per task during the meta-training stage (2-way k-shot). The meta-learning tasks are sampled on the fly during meta-training with minimum overlap. We meta-trained the model with 4000 meta-epochs, the size of batch of tasks for every meta-epoch is set to 4, i.e. after the training of 4 tasks sampled from $D_{meta-train}$, the meta-update is performed with a learning rate equal to 0.01. Adam optimizer is used with a learning rate equal to 0.01 and 10 epochs for the base-learner training.

-**Meta-testing:** The fine-tuning of the model during meta-testing stage is performed with images corresponding to each of the new classes (unseen during meta-training). The value of k in our experiments is set to 3 then to 5 indicating 2-way 3-shot and 2-way 5-shot classification respectively. During meta-test, the inference is performed by randomly sampling tasks of k images from 2 classes from $D_{meta-test}$ (rare diseases detection). The training is performed using stochastic gradient descent with a learning rate of 0.01 for 15 epochs. We compute the average Accuracy and average Area Under the Curve (AUC) across meta-test tasks.

4.2 Few-Shot Diseases Detection Results

Tables 1 and 2 represent the average Accuracy (Avg. Acc) and the average AUC (Avg. AUC) for 2-way 3-shot and 2-way 5-shot classification results for both low prevalence disease detection problems. We report 84.3% and 73.4% 2-way 5-shot classification Avg. AUC for respectively few-shot skin and few-shot thorax disease detection.

Table 1. Few-shot skin disease diagnosis from ISIC 2018 dataset (Problem 1)

	2-way 3-shot		2-way 5-shot	
	Avg. Acc	Avg. AUC	Avg. Acc	Avg. AUC
MAML [16]	73%	75.1%	77.9 %	80.1%
Transfer Learning (DenseNet)	61.12%	65.3 %	66.8%	71.5%
MetaMed [21]	75.37%	NA	78.25%	NA
Reptile [28]	73.4%	73.1%	76.2%	79.6%
Prototypical network [28]	73.5%	75.8%	79.7%	82.9%
DAML [19]	NA	79.6%	NA	83.3%
Proposed method	**76.9%**	**80.1%**	**81.9%**	**84.3 %**

In order to validate the effectiveness of our approach, we compare it with baseline methods. First, we perform transfer learning (fine-tuning) using DenseNet pre-trained model [30]. We use geometric data augmentation for both training and testing phases. Transfer learning achieves a 2-way 5-shot Avg. AUC of 71.5% and 47% for receptively problem 1 and problem 2 which are very lower than our obtained results (84.3% and 73.4%) under the same FSL settings. Transfer learning is not optimal for medical image classification problem in low data regime due to the huge difference between the learned features of real-world images (DenseNet model) and the medical images. Second, the proposed self-attention augmented MAML outperforms the baseline MAML [16] for both Avg. AUC of 2-way 3-shot and 2-way 5-shot by 4% for problem 1 and about $(4 - 6\%)$ for problem 2. Indeed, the self-attention mechanism enables the model to focus more on semantically important features and clinically relevant context. We compare the obtained classification results with SOTA few-shot classification approaches. For the dermatological disease detection task, proposed framework outperforms the DAML [19] and both Reptile and Prototypical networks [28] on the ISIC 2018 dataset for both 2-way 3-shot and 2-way 5-shot settings. Yet, we obtained better results than Sing et al. [21]. The latter proposed a gradient-based method combined with data augmentation for model regularization (81.9% versus 78.25% as 2-way 5 shot classification Avg. Acc). For the thorax diseases detection task, to the best to our knowledge there is no work that has investigated

Table 2. Few-shot thorax disease diagnosis from chest X-Ray images (Problem 2)

	2-way 3-shot		2-way 5-shot	
	Avg. Acc	Avg. AUC	Avg. Acc	Avg. AUC
MAML [16]	58.6%	60.01%	66.5%	69.3%
Transfer Learning (DenseNet)	36.5%	42.3%	45.2%	47 %
Task sampling [15]	60.2%	62.1%	68.2%	70.1%
Proposed method	**63.2%**	**66.3%**	**70.28%**	**73.4%**

the use of 16 categories for few-shot classification. Most of the existing works proposed FSL approaches for COVID-19 detection using only few categories. Hence, we propose to test the task sampling method proposed by Maicas et al. [15] in order to evaluate our method. As shown in Table 2, we obtained better results in terms of Avg. AUC and Avg. Acc for both 2-way 3-shot and 2-way 5-shot (63.2% and 70.28% of Avg. Acc respectively), while in [15], the proposed method achieved 60.2% and 68.2% of Avg. Acc respectively. Our method exploits the knowledge learned over tasks using the optimization-based meta-learning technique, as well as its ability to focus on the most relevant task-specific features (disease-specific features) through the integrated self-attention mechanism.

5 Conclusion

In this work, we proposed a few-shot disease detection method. The proposed approach is based on the meta-learning paradigm to learn from experiences and integrate a self-attention mechanism to focus on clinically relevant features. The proposed method has been evaluated on two image-based diagnosis scenarios namely low prevalence dermatological and thorax disease diagnosis. Obtained results demonstrate the effectiveness of the proposed approach compared to transfer learning and original MAML algorithm and SOTA few-shot disease detection methods. Future works include the use of under explored imaging modalities for FSL such MRI.

References

1. Chan, H.-P., Samala, R.K., Hadjiiski, L.M., Zhou, C.: Deep learning in medical image analysis. In: Lee, G., Fujita, H. (eds.) Deep Learning in Medical Image Analysis. AEMB, vol. 1213, pp. 3–21. Springer, Cham (2020). https://doi.org/10.1007/978-3-030-33128-3_1
2. Brasil, S., Pascoal, C., Francisco, R., dos Reis Ferreira, V., Videira, P.A., Valadão, G.: Artificial Intelligence (AI) in rare diseases: is the future brighter? Genes 10(12), 978 (2019)
3. Waite, S., et al.: A review of perceptual expertise in radiology-how it develops, how we can test it, and why humans still matter in the era of artificial intelligence. Acad. Radiol. 27(1), 26–38 (2020)
4. Alexander, R.G., Waite, S., Macknik, S.L., Martinez-Conde, S.: What do radiologists look for? Advances and limitations of perceptual learning in radiologic search. J. Vis. 20(10), 17 (2020)
5. Wang, Y., Yao, Q., Kwok, J.T., Ni, L.M.: Generalizing from a few examples: a survey on few-shot learning. ACM Comput. Surv. 53(3), 1–34 (2020)
6. Hospedales, T., Antoniou, A., Micaelli, P., Storkey, A.: Meta-learning in neural networks: A survey. arXiv preprint. arXiv:2004.05439 (2020)
7. Ravi, S., Larochelle, H.: Optimization as a model for few-shot learning (2016)
8. Vinyals, O., Blundell, C., Lillicrap, T., Wierstra, D., et al.: Matching networks for one shot learning. Adv. Neural. Inf. Process. Syst. 29, 3630–3638 (2016)
9. Grant, E., Finn, C., Levine, S., Darrell, T., Griffiths, T.: Recasting gradient-based meta-learning as hierarchical bayes. arXiv preprint. arXiv:1801.08930 (2018)

10. Triantafillou, E., et al.: Meta-dataset: A dataset of datasets for learning to learn from few examples. arXiv preprint. arXiv:1903.03096 (2019)
11. Makarevich, A., Farshad, A., Belagiannis, V., Navab, N.: Metamedseg: volumetric meta-learning for few-shot organ segmentation. arXiv preprint. arXiv:2109.09734 (2021)
12. Khadga, R., et al.: Few-shot segmentation of medical images based on meta-learning with implicit gradients. arXiv preprint. arXiv:2106.03223
13. Gama, P.H., Oliveira, H., dos Santos, J.A.: Weakly supervised medical image segmentation. arXiv e-prints, pp. arXiv–2108 (2021)
14. Yuan, P., et al.: Few is enough: task-augmented active meta-learning for brain cell classification. In: Martel, A.L., et al. (eds.) MICCAI 2020. LNCS, vol. 12261, pp. 367–377. Springer, Cham (2020). https://doi.org/10.1007/978-3-030-59710-8_36
15. Maicas, G., Bradley, A.P., Nascimento, J.C., Reid, I., Carneiro, G.: Training medical image analysis systems like radiologists. In: Frangi, A.F., Schnabel, J.A., Davatzikos, C., Alberola-López, C., Fichtinger, G. (eds.) MICCAI 2018. LNCS, vol. 11070, pp. 546–554. Springer, Cham (2018). https://doi.org/10.1007/978-3-030-00928-1_62
16. Finn, C., Yu, T., Zhang, T., Abbeel, P., Levine, S.: One-shot visual imitation learning via meta-learning. arXiv preprint. arXiv:1709.04905 (2017)
17. Nichol, A., Achiam, J., Schulman, J.: On first-order meta-learning algorithms. arXiv preprint. arXiv:1803.02999 (2018)
18. Snell, J., Swersky, K., Zemel, R.: Prototypical networks for few-shot learning. In: Advances in Neural Information Processing Systems, pp. 4077–4087 (2017)
19. Li, X., Yu, L., Fu, C.-W., Heng, P.-A.: Difficulty-aware meta-learning for rare disease diagnosis. arXiv preprint. arXiv:1907.00354 (2019)
20. Prabhu, V., Kannan, A., Ravuri, M., Chaplain, M., Sontag, D., Amatriain, X.: Few-shot learning for dermatological disease diagnosis. In: Machine Learning for Healthcare Conference. PMLR, pp. 532–552 (2019)
21. Singh, R., Bharti, V., Purohit, V., Kumar, A., Singh, A.K., Singh, S.K.: MetaMed: few-shot medical image classification using gradient-based meta-learning. Pattern Recogn. **120**, 108111 (2021)
22. Naren, T., Zhu, Y., Wang, M.D.: COVID-19 diagnosis using model agnostic meta-learning on limited chest x-ray images. In: Proceedings of the 12th ACM Conference on Bioinformatics, Computational Biology, and Health Informatics, pp. 1–9 (2021)
23. Shorfuzzaman, M., Hossain, M.S.: MetaCOVID: a siamese neural network framework with contrastive loss for n-shot diagnosis of COVID-19 patients. Pattern Recogn. **113**, 107700 (2020)
24. Aradhya, V.N.M., Mahmud, M., Guru, D.S., Agarwal, B., Kaiser, M.S.: One-shot cluster-based approach for the detection of COVID–19 from chest X–ray images. Cogn. Comput. **13**(4), 873–881 (2021). https://doi.org/10.1007/s12559-020-09774-w
25. Paul, A., Tang, Y.X., Shen, T.C., Summers, R.M.: Discriminative ensemble learning for few-shot chest x-ray diagnosis. Med. Image Anal. **68**, 101911 (2021)
26. Milton, M.A.A.: Automated skin lesion classification using ensemble of deep neural networks in ISIC 2018: skin lesion analysis towards melanoma detection challenge. arXiv preprint. arXiv:1901.10802 (2019)
27. Wang, X., Peng, Y., Lu, L., Lu, Z., Bagheri, M., Summers, R.M.: Chestx-ray8: Hospital-scale chest x-ray database and benchmarks on weakly-supervised classification and localization of common thorax diseases. In: Proceedings of IEEE CVPR (2017)

28. Mahajan, K., Sharma, M., Vig, L.: Meta-dermdiagnosis: few-shot skin disease identification using meta-learning. In: 2020 IEEE/CVF (CVPRW), pp. 3142–3151 (2020)
29. Cohen, J.P., Morrison, P., Dao, L., Roth, K., Duong, T.Q., Ghassemi, M.: Covid-19 image data collection: prospective predictions are the future. arXiv preprint. arXiv:2006.11988 (2020)
30. Cohen, J.P., Morrison, P., Dao, L., Roth, K., Duong, T.Q., Ghassemi, M.: Densely connected convolutional networks. In: Proceedings of the IEEE Conference on Computer Vision and Pattern Recognition, pp. 4700–4708 (2017)

Facing Annotation Redundancy: OCT Layer Segmentation with only 10 Annotated Pixels per Layer

Yanyu Xu[✉], Xinxing Xu, Huazhu Fu, Meng Wang, Rick Siow Mong Goh,
and Yong Liu

Institute of High Performance Computing, A*STAR, Singapore, Singapore
{xu_yanyu,xuxinx,fu_huazhu,wang_meng,gohsm,liuyong}@ihpc.a-star.edu.sg

Abstract. The retinal layer segmentation from OCT images is a fundamental and important task in the diagnosis and monitoring of eye-related diseases. The quest for improved accuracy is driving the use of increasingly large dataset with fully pixel-level layer annotations. But the manual annotation process is expensive and tedious, further, the annotators also need sufficient medical knowledge which brings a great burden on the doctors. We observe that there exist a large number of repetitive texture patterns in the flatten OCT images. More surprisingly, by significantly reducing the annotation from 100% to 10%, even to 1%, the performance of a segmentation model only drops a little, i.e., error from $2.53\,\mu m$ to $2.76\,\mu m$, and to $3.27\,\mu m$ on a validation set, respectively. Such observation motivates us to deeply investigate the redundancies of the annotation in the feature space which would definitely facilitate the annotation for medical images. To greatly reduce the expensive annotation costs, we propose a new annotation-efficient learning paradigm by annotating a fixed and limited number of pixels for each layer in each image. Considering the redundancies in the repetitive patterns in each layer of OCT images, we employ a VQ memory bank to store the extracted features on the whole datasets to augment the visual representation. The experimental results on two public datasets validate the effectiveness of our model. With only 10 annotated pixels for each layer in an image, our performance is very close to the previous methods trained with the whole fully annotated dataset.

Keywords: OCT layer segmentation · Annotation-efficient learning

1 Introduction

The retinal layer segmentation from retinal optical coherence tomography (OCT) images is a fundamental and important step in the diagnosis and monitor of the retinal diseases, such as diabetic retinopathy [2], glaucoma [11] and age-related macular degeneration [12]. The automatic segmentation methods has been well explored, including graph based [1,6,14], contour modeling [3,18,27], models as

X. Xu et al. (Eds.): REMIA 2022, LNCS 13543, pp. 126–136, 2022.
https://doi.org/10.1007/978-3-031-16876-5_13

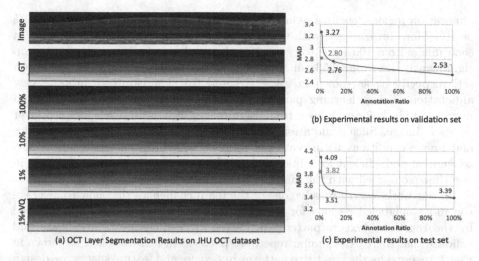

(a) OCT Layer Segmentation Results on JHU OCT dataset

(b) Experimental results on validation set

(c) Experimental results on test set

Fig. 1. An illustration of OCT layer segmentation trained on different annotation ratio training set. From top to bottom, Fig. (a) shows the flatten OCT image, ground truth layer mask, the predicted layer masks by the same network architecture using different training annotation ratio from 100%, 10% and 1%, as well as our method (1% + VQ), respectively. Figure (b) and (c) show the Mean Absolute Distance (MAD) results on validation and test set and the red points are the results of our proposed model. (Color figure online)

well as machine learning methods [1,14]. In recent years, the deep convolutional neural networks (CNNs) [8,10,17] have obtained remarkable achievements in the OCT layer segmentation task. However, the quest for improved accuracy is driving the use of large and sufficient fully annotated pixel-wise layer annotations, which is an expensive and tedious process and also needs the annotators to have medical knowledge.

Thus, we need to study how to reduce the high and expensive annotation cost via developing efficient techniques to use fewer annotations to train models and produce high performance. There exists some potential directions to reduce the annotation costs. The commonly used way is to annotate a part of full images under semi-supervised learning strategy on various medical imaging analysis, including cell segmentation [28], tumor segmentation [4], 3D abdominal CT [23], or Left Atrium segmentation [16]. Such a strategy might result in a limited number of training images, which would only include insufficient challenging scenes and degrade the model generalization ability. Some researchers employ the active learning strategy to select a part of images on brain segmentation [22] or heart, aorta segmentation [13] or patches on vessel segmentation [25], which might also meet similar challenges.

It might be redundant to annotate the whole OCT image since we observe there exist high repetitive patterns in the flatten OCT images as shown in Fig. 1 (a). Thus, we do some investigations to train the neural networks with fewer annotation regions, such as reducing the annotation rations from 100% to 10% or 1%. More surprisingly, with the great decreases of the annotated regions in each image from 100% to 10% even 1%, the model performance does not drop significantly, i.e. from $2.53\,\mu m$ to $2.76\,\mu m$, and to $3.27\,\mu m$ on the validation set, respectively, as shown in Fig. 1 (b) and (c). Therefore, we propose new annotation-efficient learning paradigm, which only needs to annotate a fixed number of pixels for each layer from each image, such as 10 pixels for each layer on each image. Such annotation ways could include more challenging scenes and image conditions to increase the models' generalization ability. It is also convenient and efficient for clinicians to click at most 100 pixels for 10 layers in one time, compared with the multiple times in the active strategy [13,22,25].

In our work, we try to solve one of the main challenges that how to leverage the most unlabeled regions for learning good visual representations. Inspired by the repetitive texture patterns in flatten OCT images, we investigate and validate that there exist similar repetitive patterns in feature space, as shown in Fig. 2. Inspired by the repetitive patterns in texture and feature spaces, we design a novel annotation-efficient learning framework based on the memory bank. In particular, we employ a VQ memory bank to store the extracted features on the whole datasets to augment the visual representation.

The contributions of this work are summarized as follows: To greatly reduce the manual annotation cost and produce competitive performance on OCT layer segmentation, we study it under a new annotation-efficient learning setting paradigm, where we only need to annotate 10 pixels for each layer on each image. Considering the redundancies in the repetitive patterns in each layer of OCT images, we employ a VQ memory bank to store the extracted features on the whole datasets to augment the visual representation. The experimental results on two public OCT layer segmentation datasets show the effectiveness of our proposed model. With only 10 annotated pixels in each layer on each image, our proposed model could achieve comparable performance with those methods based on the fully annotated training set.

2   Investigation on Less Annotated Data

2.1   Experimental Setting

We used a publicly available JHU OCT dataset [9] for the experiments. It consists of 35 human retina scans (14 are healthy controls and 21 have multiple sclerosis) acquired on a Heidelberg Spectralis SD-OCT system. Each patient has 49 B-scans with pixel size 496×1024, and 9 ground truth surfaces on each B-Scan. The z-axial resolution in each A-scan is $3.9\,\mu m$. We use an intensity gradient method [14] to flatten the retinal B-Scan image to the estimated Bruch's membrane, following [9,17,24]. The flatten B-scans are 128×1024. Following [9,24], we train the model on 5 HCs and 7 MS subjects, validate on 1 HCs and 2 MS subjects and test the remaining 20 subjects. Finally, we use the mean absolute distance (MAD) between predicted and ground truth layers to evaluate the models.

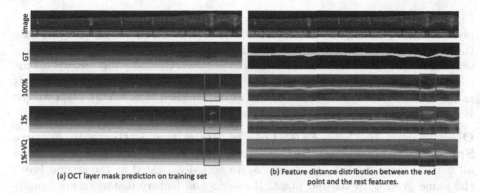

(a) OCT layer mask prediction on training set   (b) Feature distance distribution between the red
                                                         point and the rest features.

Fig. 2. An illustration of OCT layer segmentation trained on different annotation ratio training sets. Figure (a) is the flatten OCT image, ground truth layer mask, the predicted layer masks by the same network architecture using different training annotation ratios from 100%, 1%, as well as our method (1% + VQ), respectively. Figure (b) is the feature distance between the red points and the rest features on the training set. The red point located on the second layer. The features are extracted from the models using 100%, 1% annotation data and our method (1% + VQ), respectively. The yellow color means the distance is much closer, while the deep blue color means the distance is much larger. (Color figure online)

Our Aim is to Evaluate the Influence of Different Annotation Ratios for OCT Layer Segmentation Models. Rather than building a fine-tuned and top-performing segmentation model, we just used a U-Net-like architecture [15] due to its popularity, simplicity, and to minimize architectural influences on the outcomes. The architecture consists of three pooling/upsampling steps. We used a common training scheme consisting of a cross-entropy loss with Adam optimizer (learning rate: 10^{-4}). We design three baselines with different annotation ratios, using 100%, 10%, and 1%. In particular, 10% means each image is annotated 10% regions, with 128×102 pixels. Similarly, 1% means the annotation region is 128×10 pixels. The only difference is the annotation ratio in the training set.

2.2   Results and Observations

Figure 1 (b) and (c) show the MAD results of the baselines on validation and test sets. It can be observed that the model trained with more annotations would achieve better performance. However, more surprisingly, with the great decreases of the annotated regions in each image from 100% to 10% even 1%, the model performance does not drop significantly, i.e. from 0.65 to 0.71 and 0.84 on the validation set, respectively. Figure 1 (a) shows the OCT layer masks predicted by the different baselines. We can also observe that almost all models could predict the OCT layer masks, while the predicted OCT masks by the model using 1% annotation data have more noises on layer surfaces.

To deeply investigate it, we further visualize the predicted layer masks and calculate the feature distances of these models on the training set. In particular,

Fig. 2 (a) shows the flatten OCT image, ground truth layer mask, the predicted layer masks by the baselines using 100% 1% and 1%[1] Besides, we also calculate the feature distance between one feature and the rest features on the training set. Figure (b) shows the feature distances between the red point located on the second layer and the rest features. The features are extracted from the models using 100%, 1% annotation data as well as our method (1% + VQ), respectively. Based on the investigations, we have the following findings.

Observations I: There Exist Lots of Repetitive Patterns in Feature Space. As shown in Fig. 2 (b), we can see an obvious yellow belt region in all feature maps, and the belt regions are actually located at the second layer, the same layer with the red point. It means the feature distances are usually small within the same OCT layer, such as the yellow regions in all baselines. Further, we can conclude that there exist repetitive patterns in feature spaces, which result from the repetitive texture in the input OCT images. More importantly, the repetitive features models could enable the models with 100% or 1% annotation data to predict much accurately in most regions. Thus, it might be the important reason that the model trained with 1% still could achieve high performance. It also might be redundant to annotate all regions.

Observations II: The Errors Mainly Results from the Abnormal Regions. The red boxes in Fig. 2 show abnormal regions where several layers occur very close, which are the bad cases predicted by the model using 1% annotation data. We can see that in the fourth row in Fig. 2 (b), the feature distances within the red boxes are much larger than others in the third row. It means that for these abnormal or bad regions within the red boxes, the model using 1% annotation data might not learn useful visual features and results in bad predictions. Besides, we can see that in the fifth row in Fig. 2 (b), the feature distances within the red boxes are similar to the second row. Our model employs a VQ memory bank to store the feature from the whole dataset, which could further augment the learned features. We will detail this part in Sect. 3.

3   Annotation-Efficient Learning

In this work, we mainly address the OCT layer segmentation under an annotation-efficient learning network. For each OCT image $I \in \mathbb{R}^{1 \times H \times W}$, we only randomly annotate a vertical patch of $H \times 10$ area in Fig. 3. The task is to learn a deep neural network to achieve a good predictive performance on the limited annotation. As mentioned, one of the main challenges is how to extract as much as possible useful visual representation from both of them. Only limited images contain partially annotated regions and the rest images are unannotated. In this work, we propose a new memory-based annotation-efficient learning framework in Fig. 3. The whole pipeline includes feature extraction and VQ memory bank.

---

[1] '1% + VQ' is our proposed model and more details would be described in Sect. 3.

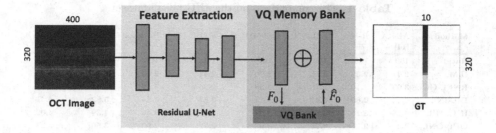

Fig. 3. An Illustration of the pipeline.

Feature Extraction: Firstly, we use a residual U-Net [15] to extract the features from retinal OCT images. It has three 2×2 max-pooling and 64 channels for all intermediate features. If the size of the input patch is $H \times W$, the feature map F_0^s extracted from the backbone is the same as the inputs. We can replace the residual U-Net with any specific state-of-the-art structure since our work does not focus on designing the best network for OCT layer segmentation.

VQ Memory Bank: Motivated by the repetitive patterns, we use the VQ memory bank to store common features. Similar to VQVAE [21,26], the memory bank E encodes and stores the labelled visual features in the whole dataset. The memory bank E is defined as a latent vector dictionary $E := e_1, e_2, ..., e_n$ where $e_i \in R^{1 \times 64}$ denotes the stored feature in the dictionary and $n = 512$ is the total size of the memory.

The feature map F_0 is used to update the VQ memory bank and retrieve an augmented feature $\hat{F}_0$. In particular, for each spatial location f_j in F_0, we find the nearest feature e_i in the VQ memory bank, via the L2 distance measure

$$\hat{f}_j = e_i, i = \arg\min_k \|f_j - e_k\|_2^2. \tag{1}$$

Following [21], we use vector quantization, a dictionary learning algorithm to learn the memory bank. The VQ loss includes

$$L_{VQ} = \|\mathrm{sg}[f] - e\|_2^2 + \|f - \mathrm{sg}[\hat{e}]\|_2^2, \tag{2}$$

where sg represents the stopgradient operator. The first loss item is used to update the memory bank, by moving the embedding vector e_i towards the encoder feature f_i. The second one is to make the encoder commits to an embedding and its output does not grow.

Loss Function: For vessel segmentation task, we adopt the commonly used pixel-wise cross entropy loss on the annotated regions $L_s = -\sum_i p^v \log(R(I^v))$, where $R(I^v)$ is the segmentation mask prediction and p^v is the partial labeled ground truth of image i. Finally, our loss function is calculated as $L = L_s + \lambda_{VQ} L_{VQ}$, where λ_{VQ} is hyper weights with $\lambda_{VQ} = 0.1$.

Table 1. The comparison on the JHU OCT dataset.

Method	AURA [14]	R-Net [7]	ReLayNet [20]	ShortPath [8]	FCBR [8]	Backbone	Label-Only	Ours
Ratio	100	100	100	100	100	100	1	1
ILM	2.37	2.38	3.17	2.70	2.41	2.65	3.48	3.13
RNFL-GCL	3.09	3.10	3.75	3.38	2.96	3.47	5.96	4.31
IPL-INL	3.43	2.89	3.42	3.11	2.87	3.84	5.82	4.41
INL-OPL	3.25	3.15	3.65	3.58	3.19	3.46	4.39	4.02
OPL-ONL	2.96	2.76	3.28	3.07	2.72	2.92	3.60	3.23
ELM	2.69	2.65	3.04	2.86	2.65	3.78	4.55	5.84
IS-OS	2.07	2.10	2.73	2.45	2.01	2.88	2.26	2.24
OS-RPE	3.77	3.81	4.22	4.10	3.55	3.86	4.00	4.35
BM	2.89	3.71	3.09	3.23	3.10	3.65	3.08	2.91
Overall	2.95	2.95	3.37	3.16	2.83	3.39	4.09	3.82

4   Experiment

4.1   Experiment Setting

We use the PyTorch [19] platform to implement our model with the following parameter settings: mini-batch size (8), learning rate (1.0e−4), momentum (0.95), weight decay (0.0005), and the number of epochs (40). We employ the default initialization to initialize the model.

We use two public datasets. The SD-OCT dataset [5] includes both 265 normal and 115 age-related macular degeneration (AMD) cases. There are three layers, including the inner limiting membrane (ILM), the inner aspect of the retinal pigment epithelium drusen complex (IRPE), and the outer aspect of Bruch's membrane (OBM). The physical resolutions are $3.24\,\mu m$ (within A-scan), $6.7\,\mu m$ (cross A-scan), and $0.067\,mm$ (cross B-scan). Following [17], we train the model on 263 subjects and test on the other 72 subjects. We also use The JHU OCT dataset [9] and the same experimental setting described in Sect. 2.1.

Following [9,17,24], we use an intensity gradient method [14] to flatten the retinal B-Scan image to the estimated Bruch's membrane. We use the mean absolute distance (MAD) as the evaluation metric.

4.2   Performance Comparison

Baselines. Since this is the first work to study the OCT layer segmentation task, we compare our model with the following methods. We use some recent state-of-the-art fully-supervised learning methods for OCT layer segmentation, which use all samples as training, such as AURA [14], R-Net [7], ReLayNet [20], FCBR [8], 2D-3D Net [17], and so on. We also design a simple baseline, 'Label-Only', directly using the partially annotated images.

We use 'Ratio' to indicate the annotated regions percentage in the training dataset. The fully-supervised methods use 100% annotated data. The 1% in JHU

Table 2. The ablation studies on the ROSE-1 (SVC) dataset. **The Left**:The comparison on the SD-OCT dataset. **The Right**: The visualization of VQ indices, generated pseudo labels and its uncertain mask on the training set.

Method	FCBR[8]	2D-3D Net[17]	Backbone	Label-Only	Ours
Ratio	100	100	100	2.5	2.5
ILM (AMD)	1.73	1.76	1.93	7.39	3.08
ILM (Normal)	1.24	1.26	1.27	3.84	1.93
IRPE (AMD)	3.09	3.04	3.47	5.88	5.61
IRPE (Normal)	2.06	2.10	2.36	3.31	2.89
OBM (AMD)	4.94	4.43	4.68	13.78	6.86
OBM (Normal)	2.28	2.40	2.30	5.44	2.91
Overall	2.78	2.71	2.91	7.45	4.34

OCT dataset means all training images include $H \times 10$ pixels annotated regions. For SD-OCT dataset, the ratio is 2.5% ($10/W = 400$).

The experimental results on the JHU OCT and SD-OCT datasets are shown on the Tables 1 and 2 Left, respectively. We can see that the baseline models 'Label-Only' could still achieve quite high performance, only using 1 % or 2.5% annotated regions, with the help of the repetitive patterns. Besides, our proposed model could achieve a performance improvement, which is close to the fully supervised FCBR, where the gap is less than 1 μm on the metric of MAD on the JHU OCT dataset. It indicates the effectiveness of the OCT layer segmentation only using 10 pixels for each layer in each image.

4.3 Ablation Study

We do the ablation study to evaluate the memory module on the JHU OCT dataset. We design the following baseline, adding the memory bank on the residual U-Net backbone. The qualitative and quantitative results are as shown in Fig. 1. The model using our proposed memory bank achieves higher performance than the backbone. The MAD result on the validation set is much close to the result of the model using 10% annotation data. It indicates that memory could store the visual representations and augment the features.

5   Discussion and Conclusion

In this work, we mainly study a new annotation-efficient setting of OCT layer segmentation with fixed and limited pixels for each layer on each image. Its goal is to reduce the annotation cost. Targeting it, we propose a new memory bank-based framework. We use the VQ memory bank to store the extracted features on the whole dataset to augment the visual representation. With 10 annotated pixels for each layer on each image, our proposed model always outperforms recent methods under semi-supervised or active learning.

Besides, the learned VQ memory bank provides more promising and potential directions to further reduce the annotation cost and improve the model performance. In the right part in Table 2, we visualize the VQ indices of the retrieved features, the generated pseudo labels, and their uncertain mask on the training set. We can see that only by annotating 10 pixels for each layer, the model could learn the relationship between features and generate much more reasonable pseudo labels. The uncertain mask of the pseudo labels is mainly located at the layer surfaces. With the help of a memory bank, we would annotate 10 pixels in fewer images rather than all images, design a new active learning framework to select and annotate these uncertain regions to further reduce the annotation costs.

Acknowledge. This research was supported by A*STAR AI3 HTPO Seed Fund (Grant No. C211118014) and the Agency for Science, Technology and Research (A*STAR) AME Programmatic Funds (Grant Number: A20H4b0141).

References

1. Antony, B.J., et al.: A combined machine-learning and graph-based framework for the segmentation of retinal surfaces in SD-OCT volumes. Biomed. Opt. Express **4**(12), 2712–2728 (2013)
2. Bavinger, J.C., et al.: The effects of diabetic retinopathy and pan-retinal photocoagulation on photoreceptor cell function as assessed by dark adaptometry. Invest. Ophthalmol. Vis. Sci. **57**(1), 208–217 (2016)
3. Carass, A., Lang, A., Hauser, M., Calabresi, P.A., Ying, H.S., Prince, J.L.: Multiple-object geometric deformable model for segmentation of macular OCT. Biomed. Opt. Express **5**(4), 1062–1074 (2014)
4. Fang, K., Li, W.-J.: DMNet: difference minimization network for semi-supervised segmentation in medical images. In: Martel, A.L., et al. (eds.) MICCAI 2020. LNCS, vol. 12261, pp. 532–541. Springer, Cham (2020). https://doi.org/10.1007/978-3-030-59710-8_52
5. Farsiu, S., et al.: Quantitative classification of eyes with and without intermediate age-related macular degeneration using optical coherence tomography. Ophthalmology **121**(1), 162–172 (2014)
6. Garvin, M.K., Abramoff, M.D., Wu, X., Russell, S.R., Burns, T.L., Sonka, M.: Automated 3-D intraretinal layer segmentation of macular spectral-domain optical coherence tomography images. IEEE Trans. Med. Imaging **28**(9), 1436–1447 (2009)
7. He, Y., et al.: Topology guaranteed segmentation of the human retina from OCT using convolutional neural networks. arXiv preprint arXiv:1803.05120 (2018)
8. He, Y., et al.: Fully convolutional boundary regression for retina OCT segmentation. In: Shen, D., et al. (eds.) MICCAI 2019. LNCS, vol. 11764, pp. 120–128. Springer, Cham (2019). https://doi.org/10.1007/978-3-030-32239-7_14
9. He, Y., Carass, A., Solomon, S.D., Saidha, S., Calabresi, P.A., Prince, J.L.: Retinal layer parcellation of optical coherence tomography images: data resource for multiple sclerosis and healthy controls. Data Brief **22**, 601–604 (2019)
10. He, Y., Carass, A., Zuo, L., Dewey, B.E., Prince, J.L.: Self domain adapted network. In: Martel, A.L., et al. (eds.) MICCAI 2020. LNCS, vol. 12261, pp. 437–446. Springer, Cham (2020). https://doi.org/10.1007/978-3-030-59710-8_43

11. Kansal, V., Armstrong, J.J., Pintwala, R., Hutnik, C.: Optical coherence tomography for glaucoma diagnosis: an evidence based meta-analysis. PLoS ONE **13**(1), e0190621 (2018)

12. Keane, P.A., et al.: Evaluation of optical coherence tomography retinal thickness parameters for use in clinical trials for neovascular age-related macular degeneration. Invest. Ophthalmol. Vis. Sci. **50**(7), 3378–3385 (2009)

13. Khan, S., Shahin, A.H., Villafruela, J., Shen, J., Shao, L.: Extreme points derived confidence map as a cue for class-agnostic interactive segmentation using deep neural network. In: Shen, D., et al. (eds.) MICCAI 2019. LNCS, vol. 11765, pp. 66–73. Springer, Cham (2019). https://doi.org/10.1007/978-3-030-32245-8_8

14. Lang, A., et al.: Retinal layer segmentation of macular oct images using boundary classification. Biomed. Opt. Express **4**(7), 1133–1152 (2013)

15. Li, D., Dharmawan, D.A., Ng, B.P., Rahardja, S.: Residual U-Net for retinal vessel segmentation. In: 2019 IEEE International Conference on Image Processing (ICIP), pp. 1425–1429. IEEE (2019)

16. Li, S., Zhang, C., He, X.: Shape-aware semi-supervised 3D semantic segmentation for medical images. In: Martel, A.L., et al. (eds.) MICCAI 2020. LNCS, vol. 12261, pp. 552–561. Springer, Cham (2020). https://doi.org/10.1007/978-3-030-59710-8_54

17. Liu, H., et al.: Simultaneous alignment and surface regression using hybrid 2D-3D networks for 3D coherent layer segmentation of retina OCT images. In: de Bruijne, M., et al. (eds.) MICCAI 2021. LNCS, vol. 12908, pp. 108–118. Springer, Cham (2021). https://doi.org/10.1007/978-3-030-87237-3_11

18. Novosel, J., Vermeer, K.A., De Jong, J.H., Wang, Z., Van Vliet, L.J.: Joint segmentation of retinal layers and focal lesions in 3-D OCT data of topologically disrupted retinas. IEEE Trans. Med. Imaging **36**(6), 1276–1286 (2017)

19. Paszke, A., et al.: PyTorch: an imperative style, high-performance deep learning library. In: Wallach, H., Larochelle, H., Beygelzimer, A., dAlché-Buc, F., Fox, E., Garnett, R. (eds.) Advances in Neural Information Processing Systems, vol. 32, pp. 8024–8035. Curran Associates, Inc. (2019)

20. Roy, A.G., et al.: ReLayNet: retinal layer and fluid segmentation of macular optical coherence tomography using fully convolutional networks. Biomed. Opt. Express **8**(8), 3627–3642 (2017)

21. Van Den Oord, A., Vinyals, O., et al.: Neural discrete representation learning. In: NeurIPS (2017)

22. Wang, G., Aertsen, M., Deprest, J., Ourselin, S., Vercauteren, T., Zhang, S.: Uncertainty-guided efficient interactive refinement of fetal brain segmentation from stacks of MRI slices. In: Martel, A.L., et al. (eds.) MICCAI 2020. LNCS, vol. 12264, pp. 279–288. Springer, Cham (2020). https://doi.org/10.1007/978-3-030-59719-1_28

23. Wang, Y., et al.: Double-uncertainty weighted method for semi-supervised learning. In: Martel, A.L., et al. (eds.) MICCAI 2020. LNCS, vol. 12261, pp. 542–551. Springer, Cham (2020). https://doi.org/10.1007/978-3-030-59710-8_53

24. Xie, H., et al.: Globally optimal segmentation of mutually interacting surfaces using deep learning. arXiv preprint arXiv:2007.01259 (2020)

25. Xu, Y., et al.: Partially-supervised learning for vessel segmentation in ocular images. In: de Bruijne, M., et al. (eds.) MICCAI 2021. LNCS, vol. 12901, pp. 271–281. Springer, Cham (2021). https://doi.org/10.1007/978-3-030-87193-2_26

26. Xu, Y., et al.: Crowd counting with partial annotations in an image. In: Proceedings of the IEEE/CVF International Conference on Computer Vision, pp. 15570–15579 (2021)

27. Yazdanpanah, A., Hamarneh, G., Smith, B., Sarunic, M.: Intra-retinal layer segmentation in optical coherence tomography using an active contour approach. In: Yang, G.-Z., Hawkes, D., Rueckert, D., Noble, A., Taylor, C. (eds.) MICCAI 2009. LNCS, vol. 5762, pp. 649–656. Springer, Heidelberg (2009). https://doi.org/10.1007/978-3-642-04271-3_79
28. Zhou, Y., Chen, H., Lin, H., Heng, P.-A.: Deep semi-supervised knowledge distillation for overlapping cervical cell instance segmentation. In: Martel, A.L., et al. (eds.) MICCAI 2020. LNCS, vol. 12261, pp. 521–531. Springer, Cham (2020). https://doi.org/10.1007/978-3-030-59710-8_51

Author Index

Printed in the United States
by Baker & Taylor Publisher Services